THE KING'S A BEGGAR

A Study of Shakespeare's Epilogues

DAVID YOUNG

ARCHWAY
PUBLISHING

Author photo by Rosen-Jones Photography

Archway Publishing books may be ordered through booksellers or by contacting:

Archway Publishing
1663 Liberty Drive
Bloomington, IN 47403
www.archwaypublishing.com
1 (888) 242-5904

ISBN: 978-1-4808-4904-4 (sc)
ISBN: 978-1-4808-4905-1 (hc)
ISBN: 978-1-4808-4906-8 (e)

Library of Congress Control Number: 2017911270

Print information available on the last page.

Archway Publishing rev. date: 08/16/2017

CONTENTS

PREFACE

This short study of Shakespeare's epilogues has had several sources and motivations. One is personal understanding. Twice I have acted in plays with epilogues and each time the experience has been intriguing. When I played the King of France in *All's Well That Ends Well*, I had the assignment of speaking the epilogue, which begins "The King's a beggar now the play is done." This is a king who has been well meaning but very authoritarian in unfortunate ways, so that his "fall" from king to humble beggar is an interesting development. But "fall" must be in quotes because the transformation is not part of the story. It happens outside and beyond, as a kind of afterthought.

So I have been an actor who steps into that in-between space that can occur between a play's close and an audience's overall response. Let's call it a *liminal* space, a term that anthropologists have developed for describing and studying rites of passage. Brides, for example, perform certain superstitions (something old, something new, something borrowed, something blue) to protect them during the transition state from maid to wife. In a liminal space, between two identities, there is a sense of risk and instability. Because plays are performed within a special boundary, originally a sacred space and still carrying overtones of magic and superstition, stepping into that boundary and speaking an epilogue before returning to one's normal identity gives the actor an odd sense of risk. My player-king experience, including my "fall," was quite memorable. It felt a little strange to be both the King and myself, David Young, at that moment. Perhaps by being both I was neither, my sense of self too blurred just then to feel valid.

Even more memorable was being in a production of *The Tempest* with Patrick Stewart and watching, close-up, as he struggled to get Prospero's epilogue to align with the rest of his performance and interpretation of the part and the play. The liminal space troubled him; moreover, he had the task of speaking Shakespeare's most important and memorable epilogue, no small assignment.

I'll close this study with an account of that experience and what I think I learned from it. Meanwhile, though, I want to outline a larger motivation than the one just described. It is curiosity about Shakespeare. While epilogues are rare in his work, the ones we have (some may not have been preserved, as I'll suggest) can be intriguing. After all, they bring us the author's perspective in a more direct fashion than was the case with the plays they conclude. Since we are naturally curious about Shakespeare's thoughts and attitudes as a working actor and playwright, might not these moments of stepping out from the story to address the audience directly give us some direct insight into what he was thinking and what he was like as a person? The point is not that he necessarily spoke the epilogues himself (though in some cases he might have, as we'll see). It's rather that there were times when he felt the necessity of direct address to the audience and broke his usual habit of ending his plays "inside the story."

I think my exploration of the surviving epilogues does reveal some interesting insights into Shakespeare's mind and art, and I have structured my survey chronologically, as a sort of crescendo toward the best of these insights. I'll begin with a chapter on typical Shakespearean endings, to establish a baseline against which the less typical choice of an epilogue can be measured. Along the way I will find myself dealing with other choric moments, especially prologues, but I will treat these only as they are germane to my primary subject, the relatively rare but crucial epilogues.

The epilogues usually tell us things we might have thought or known otherwise, but they deliver them with a particular clarity and force that I think will prove enlightening. A lifetime of teaching and writing about Shakespeare lies behind this study (the acting was quite incidental but not without its usefulness), and as both a Shakespeare scholar and a working poet, I hope to bring my imagination and experience to bear in a way that will reward attention.

INTRODUCTION: BEGINNINGS AND ENDINGS

We might begin by distinguishing between the function of prologues and epilogues. Both are external to the dramatic action, and Shakespeare and his contemporaries employed both from time to time. The prologue to *Romeo and Juliet*, for example, is this excellent sonnet:

Two households, both alike in dignity,
In fair Verona, where we lay our scene,
From ancient grudge break to new mutiny,
Where civil blood makes civil hands unclean.
From forth the fatal loins of these two foes,
A pair of star-crossed lovers take their life,
Whose misadventured piteous overthrows
Doth with their death bury their parents' strife.
The fearful passage of their death-marked love,
And the continuance of their parents' rage—
Which, but their children's end, nought could remove—
Is now the two hours' traffic of our stage;
The which, if you with patient ears attend,
What here shall miss, our toil shall strive to mend. (1–14)

This frames the story skillfully and economically. There's no boasting, but rather an attractive modesty about the whole enterprise, especially in the closing couplet. The players propose a contract: in exchange for patient attention they will work hard to make the story effective. The modesty does not reflect insecurity. A quiet confidence underlies every line. This confidence, I submit, is Shakespeare's characteristic voice as an author, communicating directly with his audience. He speaks for the company of players he is a part of, and he knows his business.

The difference between a prologue like this—along with other forms of direct address from player to audience, soliloquy and aside, that were characteristic of the period—and an epilogue is that an epilogue is more clearly outside or beyond the action, a definite afterword or afterthought. The actor who is speaking is not only addressing the audience directly but also speaking in his own person, as a member of the company and a representative of the author, emphasizing closure and signing off.

There might be many reasons for the inclusion of such after-speeches. They could address the audience especially on behalf of the company, of the author, or both. They could advertise (next week we'll be presenting X), apologize (if you expected Y, sorry that we gave you Z instead), or boast (you just saw the best play in town; go tell your friends who missed it).

The *Romeo and Juliet* Chorus will reappear at the beginning of the second act, in a similar vein—also a sonnet, but not nearly so admirable; its authorship has even been questioned—but not thereafter. The play apparently requires no epilogue, having instead the summary verse—the second half of a sonnet—from Prince Escalus:

A glooming peace this morning with it brings;
The sun for sorrow will not show his head.
Go hence to have more talk of these sad things—

Some shall be pardoned and some punished—
For never was a story of more woe
Than this of Juliet and her Romeo. (5.3.305-10)

This is a characteristic Shakespearean closure: still inside the action and the story, a figure of authority with an overview sums up the sense of the ending and, as here, anticipates a review of what has happened among the people who are still reacting to climactic events. In a tragedy there is usually a tribute to the tragic hero and the promise of an appropriate funeral, except in Macbeth's case. The distribution of justice, as here, is a typical feature as well. A play that has a prologue, then, may need no epilogue. A framing device or gesture that is preliminary does not necessitate a similar moment at the close. Some plays have both, like *Troilus and Cressida*, and two plays, *Henry V* and *Pericles*, have a chorus throughout. But I intend to leave Shakespeare's prologues to one side and to concentrate on his endings and on the infrequent variation of endings where he seems to require an epilogue.

*

At the close of a Shakespeare history play there is typically a summary of what the play's action has meant for the welfare of the nation. When the play is a part of one of his multi-play chronicle sequences, the summarizing statement can also act as a bridge to the next play. It can have ironic force, as with this close to *3 Henry VI*, spoken by King Edward, the triumphant Yorkist:

And now what rests but that we spend the time
With stately triumphs, mirthful comic shows,
Such as befits the pleasure of the court.
Sound drums and trumpets! Farewell, sour annoy!
For here I hope begins our lasting joy. (5.7.42-46)

Since the audience has been privy to his brother Gloucester's soliloquies and asides, they know that worse times are ahead for England and lasting joy is a long way off. This close functions less as a summary and more as a preview of coming attractions, in this case *Richard III*. I recall a production where, following this speech the actor playing Gloucester stood alone behind the throne, facing the audience, and spoke the first word of the next play: "Now!"

Tragedies, as I noted earlier, tend to be similar to histories in their closures, though with a stronger focus on the demise of the tragic hero and an appropriate ritual response to it: funeral rites, recognition, social restoration and restitution. In *Julius Caesar*, for example, we get a tribute to Brutus, "the noblest Roman of them all," and plans for a fitting acknowledgment of his honorable intentions from the very triumvirate who have been his enemies. At the end of *Lear*, though, Edgar feels the need for a simpler but very moving summary:

> The weight of this sad time we must obey;
> Speak what we feel, not what we ought to say.
> The oldest hath borne most; we that are young
> Shall never see so much, nor live so long.
> *Exeunt with a dead march.* (5.3.329–32)

The comedies seldom have prologues or epilogues. At the start, Shakespeare likes to plunge us right into the action with a vivid line of poetry, such as "In sooth, I know not why I am so sad" (*The Merchant of Venice*), or "If music be the food of love, play on!" (*Twelfth Night*), or "Now, fair Hippolyta, our nuptial hour / Draws on apace" (*A Midsummer Night's Dream*). Meanwhile, the close of a Shakespeare comedy typically has an umbrella statement by a character who enjoys our trust and sympathy, often accompanied by the promise of a feast, a dance, or both.

This one is typical, spoken by Valentine at the conclusion of *Two Gentlemen of Verona*:

Please you, I'll tell you as we pass along,
That you will wonder what hath fortunèd.
Come, Proteus, 'tis your penance but to hear
The story of your loves discoverèd.
That done, our day of marriage shall be yours,
One feast, one house, one mutual happiness. (5.4.165-70)

Sometimes, as in *Love's Labour's Lost* and *Twelfth Night*, there is also a concluding song. And we know that the players typically added a vigorous dance at the end, sending their audience home in a good mood.

The characteristic endings of tragedies, histories, and comedies, then, do not require epilogues, which means that an epilogue is a relatively rare phenomenon in Shakespeare's work. I note here that informal epilogues may have been relatively frequent, like the dances. But we don't know that, so we must limit ourselves to the epilogues that playscripts took the trouble to include and thereby preserve. I propose to treat seven plays that have epilogues, exploring what they may tell us about Shakespeare's practice of his art. I am excluding two late plays written in collaboration with John Fletcher, *Henry VIII* and *The Two Noble Kinsmen*, because I concur with the general view that those plays' epilogues are Fletcher's work. They simply don't sound like Shakespeare, but because they are more typical of epilogues by his contemporaries, I will treat them briefly in an appendix.

The reader may ask why there hasn't previously been a study such as this one, given all the commentary on Shakespeare over many years. The answer, I think, lies in our normal attitude toward epilogues. They often don't seem important or significant. Isn't the King of France in *All's Well* merely performing a perfunctory bow, a sort of "we hoped you liked our show, and whether or not you did we'll try to please you next time" gesture? It resembles the closing gesture in the song concluding *Twelfth Night*, when Feste finishes his verse with "A great while ago, the world begun, / With hey, ho, the wind and the rain. / But that's all one, our play is done, / And we'll strive to please you every day." This is graceful and charming, but it is not an epilogue in the full sense; Feste remains in character and, except for the glancing "we," he has not assumed the second identity of an epilogue, namely that of the actor who has played him.

Since those concluding gestures known as epilogues happen rarely in Shakespeare's plays, we do well to ask why they occur when they do. The King of France, for example, is telling us he has become a beggar. He is still speaking as the king and, at the same time, as the actor who played the king, turning from the one into the other, something like his social opposite. His authority has vanished and his role has been transformed. He is reduced from governing a country to hoping for some applause. The moment is a reflection on the nature of authority and power, an acknowledgment of their frailty and illusory existence, at once gently ironic and deeply considered.

All of Shakespeare's epilogues, I will argue, are important to our fullest understanding of the plays they belong to. Self-conscious and thoughtful, used only as absolutely necessary, they color our final response to their particular dramas, and as such, they deserve individual study and collective consideration. I am not arguing that epilogues by other dramatists are equally significant nor, on the other hand, that they are entirely negligible. What I am suggesting is that this choice on Shakespeare's part is never perfunctory and is therefore something we cannot afford to overlook if we wish to be accurately aware of his theatrical and dramatic practice. Our full sense of his art is in question, and the epilogues can tell us, I think, a good deal about that.

Actors with whom I've discussed the phenomenon of epilogues admit to being made uneasy by them. They like either to be in character or out of it, done with the part and out of, and moving away from, the play. When they stand in that liminal space where epilogues are spoken, it is hard for them to be sure of their status. Is Puck still Puck, all the way through his epilogue? If so, then he is different from the King of France, who clearly tells us he's no longer king.

But Shakespeare, obviously, did not write epilogues to make himself or his actors feel uneasy. He did it to respond to conditions and contexts surrounding particular performances, and he did it, as we will see, to underline thematic strains or elements in the play that he wanted to make sure audiences understood. He never did it casually, or boastfully, or even apologetically, as did many other playwrights. When he made the choice, he was sure of his ground, as we will see.

1. WE SHADOWS

A Midsummer Night's Dream, 1595

The first epilogue we come across when we move chronologically through Shakespeare's work is the one that Puck speaks at the end of *A Midsummer Night's Dream*. This play belongs to 1595. It marks the second year of Shakespeare's newly stable creative situation as resident shareholder, playwright, and player with the recently formed company known as the Chamberlain's Men. As numerous commentators have noticed (Bart Van Es in particular), the new situation for the playwright and his players, as reflected in the plays of 1594-95, *Richard II*, *Love's Labour's Lost*, *Romeo and Juliet*, and *Dream*, marked a step forward in Shakespeare's dramaturgy. He developed a more distinctive and less rhetorical poetic style. He began to generate drama from the developing interrelationships of characters rather than by setting up static or stereotyped figures and situations. He grew less dependent on his fellow playwrights for his models and his style, displaying a willingness to experiment with new possibilities of dramatic form. Each of the four plays from this period is constructed along new lines in terms of their predecessors among history plays, tragedies, and comedies, both those of Shakespeare himself and of his contemporary playwrights (Marlowe, Kyd, Peele, Nashe, Greene) in the first half of the 1590s.

The reconsideration of dramatic structure is partly reflected through self-referential features. There are scenes that are evocatively theatrical, full of staging and role-playing, such as the abdication scene in *Richard II* and the Capulet masquerade in *Romeo and Juliet*. Even more to the point, we also begin to have plays within plays, first in the Pageant of the Nine Worthies that concludes *Love's Labour's Lost* and then, more fully and delightfully, with the group of mechanicals who rehearse and perform *Pyramus and Thisbe* for the marriage of Theseus and Hippolyta. We watch the mechanicals meet to distribute parts and schedule their rehearsal, we watch the rehearsal in the forest, interrupted by Bottom's transformation, and we see in the last act the performance itself, with its own audience and its own mixture of abysmal failure and accidental success—it fails as a tragedy but turns out to be hugely amusing.

The embedded theatrical venture in *Dream* invites the audience to consider the process by which plays are written, cast, rehearsed and performed, and it is the ineptitude of Quince and Bottom and the rest of their players, at every stage, that allows us to measure and understand the degree of professional success that Shakespeare and his company have achieved. The inept play within the skilled play acts as a mirror of our own experience and thus lets us consider the nature of drama, acting, and poetry.

The innovative structure of *A Midsummer Night's Dream* juxtaposes two worlds, the daytime one of Theseus' Athens and the nighttime forest realm of Oberon, Titania, and the fairies. The alternation of these settings allows them to comment on each other, and the night realm tends to surround the daytime world just as the forest surrounds Athens. The Athenians may suppose that the forest is a disordered wilderness, but while it does contain the consequential quarrels of the fairy king and queen and the mischief and transformations of Puck, it is ultimately associated with creativity and imagination, an indispensable source of human wonder and delight. Wilderness and art display their deep affinity.

We open in the daylight world and then transfer to the forest for the main action of the play. The return to Athens, for the weddings and then the entertainment of the mechanicals, serves to sharpen our sense of Theseus' limited understanding of his relation to art and to nature. When he and Hippolyta discuss the adventures of the lovers, he is sure he can dismiss them as insubstantial dreams or fantasies:

> More strange than true. I never may believe
> These antique fables, nor these fairy toys.
> Lovers and madmen have such seething brains,
> Such shaping fantasies, that apprehend more
> Than cool reason ever comprehends.
> The lunatic, the lover, and the poet
> Are of imagination all compact.
> One sees more devils than vast hell can hold;
> That is the madman. The lover, all as frantic,
> Sees Helen's beauty in a brow of Egypt.
> The poet's eye, in a fine frenzy rolling,
> Doth glance from heaven to earth, from earth to heaven.
> And as imagination bodies forth
> The forms of things unknown, the poet's pen
> Turns them to shapes and gives to aery nothing
> A local habitation and a name. (5.1.2–17)

We're delighted to have a figure from mythology reject myth ("antic fables") and hear a dramatic character tell us his existence is fundamentally meaningless ("aery nothing"). Imagination here pretends to dismiss itself by way of mounting an affirmation of its singular power and validity, along with a sly critique of reason. Hippoloyta's response proves wiser:

> But all the story of the night told over,
> And all their minds transfigured so together,
> More witnesseth than fancy's images
> And grows to something of great constancy;
> But, howsoever, strange and admirable. (23–27)

Shakespeare was ready to write a kind of defense of imagination, especially as it involved itself with playing, poetry, and such kindred activities as folklore and mythology. Working as a poet in the theater, he felt his strength and new success. He was also ready, it turns out, to write his first epilogue.

*

Bottom and his fellow mechanicals have performed and departed. The iron tongue of midnight has told twelve. The humans have gone to bed, and the fairies reappear, a symmetrical completion of the play's structure, which has alternated the human and fairy worlds and doings. The fairies have come to bless the house and the matrimonial beds of three newlywed couples. We associated them with the forest, but their power now extends to the city and the palace. Puck, their representative, is also, as Shakespeare's audience well knew, a household spirit who, when placated properly, would do human tasks and chores overnight while the household slept. We are glad to see him again, and to hear him invoke the mysteries of the night while introducing the activities of this last, ritual moment. He enters carrying a prop that helps confirm his domestic purpose, a broom:

> Now the hungry lion roars,
> And the wolf behowls the moon,

Whilst the heavy plowman snores,
All with weary task fordone.
Now the wasted brands do glow,
Whilst the screech-owl, screeching loud,
Puts the wretch that lies in woe
In remembrance of a shroud.
Now it is the time of night
That the graves, all gaping wide,
Every one lets forth his sprite,
In the churchway paths to glide;
And we fairies, that do run
By the triple Hecate's team,
From the presence of the sun,
Following darkness like a dream,
Now are frolic. Not a mouse
Shall disturb this hallowed house.
I am sent with broom before,
To sweep the dust behind the door. (357–76)

Some of this is fairly frightening. The authority and benevolence of Theseus and Athens are displaced by surrounding terrors of darkness, predatory animals, ghosts, death, and mystery. The first ten lines serve to remind the audience that the night forest they have watched the lovers and fairies cavort in can be a terrifying place. Even if hungry lions and wolves were not a problem in Elizabeth's England, the idea of gaping graves and the proximity of death was enough to make the darkness of midnight a dreadful prospect.

Yet the fairies, who also inhabit this larger realm, bring a sense of reassurance. Oberon and Titania lead their retinue in a song and dance. Then Oberon, who has earlier reminded Puck that they enjoy both darkness and daylight, speaks a blessing on the house and its inhabitants. The rest of the fairies leave, and Puck

turns back to the audience to speak an epilogue. Is he also going
to utter a charm, cast a spell? Is he speaking as Puck or is he an
actor speaking now for the company and the author? I suggest
that he is both:

> If we shadows have offended,
> Think but this, and all is mended,
> That you have but slumbered here
> While these visions did appear.
> And this weak and idle theme,
> No more yielding but a dream,
> Gentles, do not reprehend;
> If you pardon, we will mend.
> And as I am an honest puck,
> If we have unearnèd luck
> Now to 'scape the serpent's tongue,
> We will make amends ere long;
> Else the puck a liar call.
> So, good night unto you all.
> Give me your hands, if we be friends,
> And Robin shall restore amends. (409–24)

In this final moment Puck can be both a fairy and an actor, con-
futing two very different things because both have been dismissed
as "shadows," lacking real substance. Folklore and drama are
equally suspect in the rational, daylight world of Theseus, even
though he himself unwittingly belongs to classical mythology and
is merely a character in a play. Oblivious to that irony, "The best in
this kind are but shadows," he reassures Hippolyta as they prepare
to watch "Pyramus and Thisbe." We remember that Puck called
Oberon "king of shadows." Even though they are dismissed as
lacking substance, both the fairies and the actors possess a larger

perspective and seem connected to an unaccountable power. So "shadows" suddenly have a value that we would ignore at our peril. Puck's inviting us to conclude that we have been dreaming has a similarly ironic bite. As the play has proved, from its title on through much of its action, dreams are much more potent than Theseus supposes. In fact, Bottom, who has "dreamed" that he became the consort and paramour of the Fairy Queen, has a much better take on the significance that a dream can have. He wants his dream, which "has no bottom," made into art as a ballad, which in a sense is what has happened. By the time the play is done with us, as I have argued elsewhere, it has challenged our familiar binary oppositions—dreaming and waking, imagination and reason, nature and art—by reversing them and by undermining their oversimplified account of reality. Puck's sly invitation is a way of reminding us how far we have come and just how accomplished the dramatic art whose spokesman he has become has managed to be.

Under the "apology" of the epilogue, then, lies a tremendous joy in the play's creative accomplishment, challenging the audience to a new level of understanding and appreciation. "Mend" and "amend" are part of an offer to improve, given tolerance and approbation. But it is hard to imagine improving on this, one of Shakespeare's most accomplished and successful comedies.

*

A Midsummer Night's Dream feels as though it was partly written for the enjoyment it would provide at some great house, for an aristocratic family and their friends. If, for example, it was performed in honor of a marriage as many have conjectured, then the blessing at the end would have a special relevance. It would be literally the case that the fairies/actors, re-entering the great hall where the performance took place, were echoing the situation moments earlier, where the mechanicals were called upon to perform for Theseus and his court. Bottom, playing the dead Pyramus, had started up to life and addressed the Duke in his own person: "Will it please you to see the epilogue, or to hear a Bergomask dance between two of our company?" Here as elsewhere he confuses hearing and seeing. In any case, offering a choice is an interesting idea. Theseus responds kindly but firmly:

> No epilogue, I pray you; for your play needs no excuse. Never excuse, for when the players are all dead, there need none to be blamed. Marry, if he that writ it had played Pyramus and hanged himself in Thisbe's garter, it would have been a fine tragedy; and so it is, truly, and very notably discharged. But come, your Bergomask; let your epilogue alone. (5.1.342–48)

After the dance Theseus sends everyone to bed with the typical end-of-a-comedy promise: "A fortnight hold we this solemnity / In nightly revels and new jollity." That feels like the end of the play, at least in respect to the smaller compass of the human realm. But it is not the last word, as Puck and Oberon demonstrate, nor the last dance, as the fairies will show us. And they do not "leave [the] epilogue alone." It's too tempting to let the "shadows" have the last word. Puck wants to seem humble and even apologetic, as if the play "need[ed] ... excuse" while the words he speaks and the associations they gather, around the dreaming/waking, day/night, reason/imagination, shadow/substance and nature/art dichotomies are as triumphant and celebratory as anything Shakespeare wrote. His confidence is masked, by the character and by the seeming apology, but it is unmistakably present in this epilogue.

2. AT ELIZABETH'S COURT

2 Henry IV, 1598

Shakespeare was in the midst of one of his finest accomplishments, the four-play sequence that includes *Richard II, 1 Henry IV, 2 Henry IV,* and *Henry V,* when he composed the next epilogue we have from him. That he needed an epilogue was less from the urge to celebrate the achievements of play, players, and, by implication, audience, and more from a need for clarification, assurance, and even apology. For one thing, he was presenting a harsh sequel to what had been an immensely popular play. It is not just the fact that the prince will have to repudiate his friendship with Falstaff when he is crowned king. Shakespeare also wants to make his audience more fully aware of the costs and sufferings that historical struggles had involved, for all levels of society. Thus it is that the second Henry IV play puts a much greater emphasis on old age, disease, deception, and death.

In order to set the new tone, the playwright includes a prologue, spoken by Rumor, "painted full of tongues," that is clearly confrontational:

Open your ears; for which of you will stop
The vent of hearing when loud Rumor speaks?
...
                    Rumor is a pipe

> Blown by surmises, jealousies, conjectures,
> And of so easy and so plain a stop
> That the blunt monster with uncounted heads,
> The still discordant, wav'ring multitude,
> Can play upon it. But what need I thus
> My well-known body to anatomize
> Among my household? (Pro.1–2, 15–22)

This is much harsher than anything that has preceded it, in the way of prologue or epilogue. It is a strong signal for the tone of a dark but magnificent play. That the play might also need an epilogue should come as no surprise. But to discover this we need first to tease out the matter of one, two, or even three different epilogues.

Readers of Shakespeare have been rightly puzzled, for many years now, to come to the end of *2 Henry IV* and find themselves confronted with a long and rambling piece of prose, usually with the accompanying indication "*Spoken by a dancer.*" It is easy to dismiss this attachment as not particularly relevant to the play or its concluding scene, which is mainly famous for the rejection of Falstaff by his old friend Prince Hal, newly crowned as Henry V. Most readers (and most performers) decide that this epilogue must have had its origins in circumstances we have since lost track of. It is dismissed, ignored, and, so far as I know, never performed.

Part of the confusion stems from the fact that the "epilogue" is actually two epilogues, or even possibly three, jammed together by editors who did not take the trouble to differentiate them. The three paragraphs were run together, with small gaps between them, in the original Quarto and again in the Folio. Subsequent editors simply followed suit.

More recently, however, commentators and editors have begun to sort out the differences among these three paragraphs and have suggested ways in which we could better understand them. My account will reflect what I take to be the most persuasive of these recent conjectures.

First there is the matter of chronology. Here is the epilogue (the middle paragraph in that prose muddle) that was probably composed and delivered first, to close an early performance of this play. We can be reasonably certain that it was spoken by Will Kemp, the resident clown of Shakespeare's company, who would have just finished playing the part of Falstaff. Falstaff has just been rejected by the newly crowned king and seems to be headed for prison:

> If my tongue cannot entreat you to acquit me, will you command me to use my legs? And yet that were but light payment, to dance out of your debt. But a good conscience will make any possible satisfaction, and so would I. All the gentlewomen here have forgiven me; if the gentlemen will not, then the gentlemen do not agree with the gentlewomen, which was never seen before in such an assembly. (5.5.Ep.17–22)

If we take this to be Kemp, speaking partly as Falstaff and partly in his own right as a popular actor famous for the bawdy jigs he performed at the end of plays, we can say that he's asking them to accept the necessity of Hal's rejection of Falstaff and at the same time to exercise a generosity that Hal and his story were not capable of. It's an admission that the author, in putting together the four-play sequence of which this is the third, has changed the mood and tone of a hugely successful predecessor in a way that may make both the acting company and its audience nervous and distressed. In other words, Shakespeare is suggesting, through Kemp's edgy farewell, that we can assent to the necessary rejection of Falstaff while also celebrating the survival of Falstaff/Kemp, who has bounced back to continue to entertain us. It's an unusual move, an acknowledgment that Falstaff threatens to exist on his own, outside the play (as indeed he proved to do, all the way down to the present). It would be made even more striking if Kemp had to remove his false Falstaffian stomach in order to perform a dance at his usual level of capability.

Falstaff/Kemp is counting on the women in the audience for support, using a gender division as a rhetorical device to placate the men. We can't recreate the entire context of this, but we can certainly pick up on the idea that women are more forgiving and less judgmental, and that men are the ones more likely to quibble on matters of kingship and history. We have seen Falstaff inspire unwarranted affection in Mistress Quickly and Doll Tearsheet, and are amused to think that he would turn around and start wheedling and flattering the ladies in the audience, being characteristically brash and bold in the face of criticism and adversity. Behind him, of course, lurks the playwright, calculating the success of his readings of history and his risky but necessary dismissal of one of the most popular dramatic characters he had ever created. He needs and asks for assent to this whole enterprise. And he's disposed to make the women his allies in this.

That paragraph is complete in itself and most likely was the play's first epilogue. Next comes a paragraph which may be seen as its continuation, as James Shapiro argues, or as an alternative epilogue on another occasion, as Giorgio Melchiori suggests:

> One word more, I beseech you. If you be not too much cloyed with fat meat, our humble author will continue the story, with Sir John in it, and make you merry with fair Katharine of France, where, for anything I know, Falstaff shall die of a sweat, unless already 'a be killed with your hard opinions. For Oldcastle died martyr, and this is not

the man. My tongue is weary. When my legs are too, I
will bid you good night. (5.5.Ep.23–30)

The argument for seeing this as a continuation of the first paragraph stems from the way it opens, and from the continuity of
imagery. "One word more" may suggest a continuation of the
epilogue under way, but it could also, of course, be a way to begin
an epilogue after a play has just concluded. "Tongue" has been
prominent in the play from the beginning, when the prologue was
spoken by Rumor "*painted full of tongues*"; and "legs" of course
connects both paragraphs to the intention to entertain with a
dance.

We also know that the players are having to apologize to Lord
Cobham and other descendants of Sir John Oldcastle for having
given Falstaff that name, or at least alluding to it, in the first
versions of the previous play, *1 Henry IV.* Oldcastle was indeed
a friend of Hal/Henry, but he was also seen as a Lollard mar-
tyr and thus revered by Protestants. Calling him Falstaff, which
seems to be a bit of wordplay connecting to "our humble author"
(fall-staff, shake-spear), is by way of making public apology to an
important member of the Court for any confusion caused earlier.
Shakespeare seems to have adapted Falstaff's name from Fastolf,
a cowardly knight in one of the Henry VI plays.

It's as though Kemp has also been handed the task of preview-
ing the next installment in the series, the *Henry V* our humble
author is already at work on. He doesn't know exactly what he'll
be doing in the role as the story continues, but he can conjecture
about further jokes involving his fat and his cowardice.

As things turned out, Falstaff did not show up in the next
play, except to have his death described, and, not coinciden-
tally, Kemp left the company. He and Shakespeare had probably
been somewhat at artistic odds. Despite good roles—Bottom,
Dogberry, Lancelot Gobbo, and, most of all, Falstaff—Kemp

apparently continued to play Kemp as well, to exploit his celebrity and notoriety. He appears to have embroidered his parts, mugging and chatting with the audience, and this fundamental disagreement about how clowns should integrate themselves with the company and the production (something Hamlet comments on in his advice to the players) led to a parting of the ways and a new and different clown.

What happened to Falstaff along the way was that he got his own play, *The Merry Wives of Windsor*, a comedy that is traditionally attributed to the Queen's desire to see the fat knight in love. So we seem to have something like the following sequence:

- Shakespeare writes *1 Henry IV*, with spectacular success for the part of Falstaff, written for Will Kemp. But Falstaff's apparent relation to the historical Sir John Oldcastle creates a critical response among Oldcastle's descendants (who include Lord Cobham, the influential incoming Lord Chamberlain) and their friends.

- Shakespeare writes the dark sequel, *2 Henry IV*, with the rejection of Falstaff and the prologue spoken by Rumor, the epilogue spoken by Kemp (one or both of the paragraphs just examined). He promises to bring Falstaff back in the next play while also issuing an apology over the Oldcastle controversy.

- Instead, he writes *Merry Wives*, possibly at the Queen's behest, and, according to tradition, within two weeks.

- Continuing work on *Henry V*, he decides to leave Falstaff out of it, either having already parted ways with Kemp, or to provoke such a parting. The continuing discomfort around the audience responses to the Oldcastle issue and, perhaps, to an unpopular reaction to *Merry Wives* leads to yet another epilogue, for a court performance, this one very likely spoken by Shakespeare himself.

In that sequence, the two paragraphs can be seen as one epilogue, composed for Kemp, or two different epilogues fairly close
together in time, the second one necessitated by the Oldcastle
brouhaha. If two, we may imagine the second one spoken by
Kemp or, if he was out of favor or uncooperative, by some other
member of the company. If Kemp was the speaker of both paragraphs, having him mention that he did not know what was going
to happen to Falstaff ("for all I know") was Shakespeare's way of
reminding him, and the audience, who was really in charge. If he
was not given the epilogue and the ensuing dance, that would be
a clear sign of the impending split with the company.

I lean toward the notion that both paragraphs were for
Kemp, and that they were probably delivered as one epilogue.
One wonders, though, how they got their original order re-
versed, a fact that supports the theory that they were written
separately and for different performances. In any case, they reflect some troubled understandings about Falstaff, about Kemp,
and about the needs of the history sequence. They are a bump
in the road to a successful realization of the Henriad tetralogy,
as we now like to call that four-play sequence from *Richard II* to
Henry V that is so rich and varied in its treatment of historical
events and materials.

This brings us to the other (or third) epilogue, which comes
first in the order of printing (as was the case in the original Quarto
and then again in the Folio) but is now generally thought to be
the later one. Most commentators are willing to assume that it was
spoken by Shakespeare himself, a rare instance of the playwright
commenting directly on his own work. James Shapiro argues
persuasively that it was written and spoken on the occasion of a
performance for the Court at Whitehall, during the Christmas
season of 1598:

First, my fear; then my curtsy; last my speech. My fear is
your displeasure, my curtsy my duty, and my speech to
beg your pardons. If you look for a good speech now, you
undo me; for what I have to say is of mine own making,
and what, indeed, I should say will, I doubt, prove mine
own marring. But to the purpose, and so to the venture:
be it known to you, as it is very well, I was lately here in
the end of a displeasing play to pray your patience for it
and to promise you a better. I meant indeed to pay you
with this, which, if like an ill venture it come unluckily
home, I break, and you, my gentle creditors, lose. Here
I promised you I would be, and here I commit my body
to your mercies: bate me some, and I will pay you some
and, as most debtors do, promise you infinitely. And so
I kneel down before you, but, indeed, to pray for the
Queen. (5.5.Ep.1–16)

It has to be said first of all that we can't be absolutely sure that
this was spoken by Shakespeare (or even that it is the last of the
epilogues). The phrase "what I have to say is of mine own making" is usually taken as proof of the author speaking directly, but
if it refers just to the wording of the epilogue, then it is not the
author but the player, from whom we should not look for "a good
speech," since he is an actor, not a writer. The epilogue, in other
words, could be assigned to any member of the company who
had the role of apologist, for the displeasing play he had already
previously apologized for, and for the present one. If the speaker
is one of the players, then the epilogue's tone and content make a
good deal of sense. It seems uncharacteristic for Kemp, however,
since it is somber and ends not with a dance but with kneeling
and a prayer. And the trope that one of the actors has decided,
on his own, to author an epilogue seems unlikely, even if it is the
company's leading man, Burbage.

Then what if it *is* Shakespeare himself, as seems most likely, the author we are always searching for behind the masks of his dramaturgy? If that's the case, he's still being fairly circumspect, about himself, his craft, and his audience. The displeasing play might be *Merry Wives*; if so, then he's reminding them that that was a detour and that the real continuity will involve the move from this play to *Henry V.* So he kneels, as if to ask pardon, but then says he's doing it to pray for the Queen. This is the feature that suggests it was composed specifically for a Court performance. As Shapiro points out, his gesture would have meant everybody else in the room, including the disapproving Cobham and the fractious Kemp, would have to kneel and pray too.

Meanwhile, mentioning the displeasing play, if it was indeed *Merry Wives*, would serve to remind the audience, including the Queen, that the playwright was constrained by royal command, and thus pardonable. That would be a clever way of compounding the exculpability: "You didn't like *Merry Wives*? Well, God save the Queen! She did ask for it, after all. We've now revived the second Henry the Fourth play. Kemp has been on his good behavior today, but it wouldn't do to let him speak the epilogue or dance one of his bawdy jigs here at the Court. I'm keeping up my side of our contract and bargain. It's up to you to do the same. On to *Henry V.*"

But what if the "displeasing play" was the first part of *Henry IV*? The phrase "I was lately here" seems to suggest that it was at a performance in Whitehall, before the court and the Queen. And "displeasing" would surely cover Lord Cobham's reaction to the misrepresentation of his martyred ancestor Oldcastle, companion to Prince Hal. If that was the issue, then an apology to Cobham, not as overt as in the previous epilogue but spoken this time by the author himself, in front of the court and Queen, would have to be the main motive for this particular epilogue.

While these are conjectures, they certainly give us an access to some of the literary politics that surrounded the writing and staging of Shakespeare's second historical tetralogy. Once completed, stretching from *Richard II* through to *Henry V* and the Battle of Agincourt (and the outburst of patriotism that story would provoke), the group of four connected histories could be seen and admired as a major artistic accomplishment. But while its composition and performance was in process, the popular Falstaff had to be created and then disposed of, and the difficult actor Kemp had to be disciplined and then dismissed. On top of that, there was the Oldcastle embarrassment to deal with. Complications galore, in other words, necessitating these two (or three) somewhat nervous epilogues.

If the author finally had to appear in his own person, and kneel, both to ask for forgiveness and to pray for the Queen, it must have felt like a considerable, but necessary, concession to circumstances. That, I think, is our best conjecture about the state of affairs that led to the "kneeling epilogue."

Shapiro calls Shakespeare's court epilogue "brassy and confident." To me it sounds more apologetic and hesitant. Among the epilogues we'll be examining, these two (three?) from *2 Henry IV* would appear to be the most troubled: the product of turbulent circumstances both within the company and in the world at large. We can follow this thread further when we deal later on with the chorus and epilogue to *Henry V*. But it's appropriate at this point to note how different these three paragraphs are from the *Dream* epilogue. Rather than celebratory, they feel apologetic and circumstantial. Thus they demonstrate one of the ways epilogues could be used: as damage control.

*

Meanwhile, while we are on the subject of court performances for Elizabeth, let us examine another curiosity, a Shakespearean epilogue without a play. We owe the survival of this little "curtain speech" to a courtier named Henry Stanford who happened to keep a commonplace book. Stanford was attached to the household of Baron Hunsdon, who was appointed Lord Chamberlain in 1597 and was, among other things, the official patron of Shakespeare's company. Stanford jotted down an epilogue that was delivered at court before the Queen, probably on Shrove Tuesday in 1599. The date and the imagery of the epilogue suggest to me that it was delivered after a performance of *As You Like It*. It goes like this:

As the dial hand tells o'er
The same hours it had before,
Still beginning in the ending,
Circular account still lending,
So, most mighty Queen we pray
Like the dial day by day
You may lead the seasons on,
Making new when old are gone.
That the babe which now is young
And hath yet no use of tongue
Many a Shrovetide here may bow
To that Empress I do now,
That the children of these lords,
Sitting at your council boards,
May be grave and agèd seen
Of her that was their fathers' Queen.
Once I wish this wish again,
Heaven subscribe it with "Amen."

Since the Chamberlain's Men, sponsored by Hunsdon and with Shakespeare as their chief playwright, performed on that Shrove Tuesday before Lent, they almost certainly performed a play by Shakespeare, and this epilogue was most likely his as well, a graceful wish for a long life to an already elderly monarch. The talk of dial hands and seasons fits with a production of *As You Like It*, where measured time and the timeless forest coexist as strange companions. We may also be reminded of Touchstone's story, early in the play, of the knight and the pancakes, since pancakes were a Shrove Tuesday staple.

On the other hand, many commentators put the composition of *As You Like It* later, in the summer of that year when it was first mentioned in the Stationer's Register. Shapiro thus argues for a revival of *A Midsummer Night's Dream* as the court performance, this epilogue presumably displacing Puck's. Another candidate might be the recent *Much Ado About Nothing*. It's all conjecture. We are certain of the date and the performance, so the authorship attribution fits and for me, at least, *As You Like It*, perhaps an early version of the play we have come to know, comes most plausibly to mind.

It is a small miracle that this bit of occasional verse has survived to charm us as it once served to charm Elizabeth. It is very slight and if Shakespeare wrote it we can surmise that he didn't think it worth preserving. It had served its turn and could vanish. Its accidental survival points to another insight as well: it may exemplify a practice that was much more common than the handful of epilogues we happen to have would suggest. When something occasional was dashed off, perhaps for a special occasion of performance, as at the Court, it may not have stayed attached to the script that was then preserved for subsequent performances with different audiences or for eventual publication. Some of the epilogues we have, such as Puck's and Rosalind's, may in fact be occasional in just that way, attached to a specific performance at a specific place and time and preserved more by happenstance than by deliberate regard. We'll never know for sure. Whatever the answer, this epilogue aligns with the other one, in prose, addressed to the Queen and especially to Lord Cobham, from *2 Henry IV,* and makes one wonder if other court performances were similarly graced. Shakespeare's fondness for this particular meter in his epilogues is in any case not in question.

3. KING JAMES AT WILTON HOUSE

As You Like It, 1599, 1603

Among the most admired of Shakespeare's comedies, *As You Like It* belongs to 1599, meaning that it was probably written and performed within a few months of that court performance of *2 Henry IV* discussed in the previous chapter. It also happens to have an epilogue, in prose and to be spoken by the actor playing Rosalind. This epilogue was perhaps given at each public performance, but it may possibly also be unique, as we shall see, to a later revival of the play performed before King James. That performance was given at Wilton House in 1603, during the early months after James's accession to the throne. There is some reason, I think, to attribute the epilogue to that revival.

We have already seen that Shakespeare tended to give his epilogues, when he decided to include them, to his fellow actors: the actor who played Puck, the actor who played Falstaff (Kemp), and in this case, the boy who took the part of Rosalind. The exception to this practice may be the court epilogue to *2 Henry IV*, but even there we cannot be sure whether it was spoken by Shakespeare or by, for instance, the company's leading actor, Richard Burbage.

That this epilogue chooses to focus on Rosalind should not surprise us. She is unique, and so is the story of her courtship and marriage. If we consider all the pairs of lovers who are headed toward marriage at the close of Shakespearean comedies, we can observe that they are often oddly, even disquietingly, mismatched. Bertram and Helena from *All's Well*, Petruchio and Kate from *The Taming of the Shrew*, the paired-off couples in *A Midsummer Night's Dream*, Bassanio and Portia from *The Merchant of Venice*, the Duke and Isabella from *Measure for Measure*, Orsino and Viola along with Olivia and Sebastian in *Twelfth Night*—we may shake our heads in dismay, or at least misgiving. What lies ahead for these unlikely couples?

Beatrice and Benedick in *Much Ado About Nothing* give us more confidence about their future happiness, and Rosalind and Orlando, from this play, may also strike us as likely to be happy in their future life together. This despite what would seem to be a disparity in wit and intelligence: Rosalind is so inventive, wise, and quick-witted that it's hard to imagine Orlando, whose physical courage and strength of resolve are his best attributes, keeping up with her. He is no Benedick, certainly. But he makes good progress in that direction because their love is wonderfully delayed, and thus tested, by the play's relatively uneventful plot.

Shakespeare had created some excellent and resourceful women characters in previous comedies (most notably Beatrice and Portia), but his achievement with Rosalind was a new and somewhat startling accomplishment. Rosalind is able to use her disguise as a boy to construct a mock courtship, giving Orlando lessons in how to woo and bringing him from a tongue-tied and lovesick infatuation to a more realistic assessment of the often difficult relations between the sexes. Along the way her observations are stinging and memorable:

> The poor world is almost six thousand years old, and in all this time there was not any man died in his own person, *videlicet*, in a love cause.... Men have died from time

to time, and worms have eaten them, but not for love.
(4.1.82–85, 92–94)

No, no, Orlando: men are April when they woo, December
when they wed; maids are May when they are maids, but
the sky changes when they are wives. (127–30)

Make the doors upon a woman's wit, and it will out at
the casement; shut that, and 'twill out at the keyhole;
stop that, 'twill fly with the smoke out at the chimney.
(141–44)

These remarks, which are part of the disguised Rosalind's edu-
cation of her husband-to-be, are in an extremely vivacious prose,
eschewing poetry and its ready association with lovers and loving.
There is poetry in the play, of course, most notably the famous
"Seven Ages of Man" speech by Jaques, but Touchstone, the clown
who tests others by his wit and wordplay, and Rosalind, who takes
charge of events in the forest, both favor prose, not least to criticize
the bad poems that the lovesick Orlando hangs up on trees.

Touchstone's character marks the replacement of Kemp as
company clown by Robert Armin, who brought an interest in
professional fools and jesters to the Chamberlain's Men. Jaques,
who reflects a growing contemporary fashion for satire and mel-
ancholy, and who is largely out of place in the forest, is delighted
to discover him:

A fool, a fool! I met a fool i'th' forest—
A motley fool! A miserable world!
As I do live by food, I met a fool,
Who laid him down and basked him in the sun,
And railed on Lady Fortune in good terms,
In good set terms, and yet a motley fool.

"Good morrow, fool," quoth I. "No sir," quoth he,
"Call me not fool till heaven hath sent me fortune."
And then he drew a dial from his poke,
And looking on it with lackluster eye,
Says very wisely, "It is ten o'clock.
Thus we may see," quoth he, "how the world wags.
'Tis but an hour ago since it was nine,
And after one hour more 'twill be eleven.
And so from hour to hour we ripe and ripe,
And then from hour to hour we rot and rot,
And thereby hangs a tale." (2.7.12–28)

These observations about the passage of time and the measured course of human life will connect nicely to Jaques' speech about the seven ages of man. It is almost as if Touchstone, the moral fool, has inspired it, and indeed he outwits Jaques at each of their meetings. The fact that Rosalind can match wits with this clever clown and that they have a strong bond of loyalty helps validate both of them for the audience. And prose, inspired by the euphuism of Shakespeare's source *Rosalind* but transcending its well-known mannerisms and weaknesses, is their favored medium.

Small wonder, then, that when the playwright elects to have Rosalind speak an epilogue, he chooses prose:

It is not the fashion to see the lady the epilogue, but it is no more unhandsome than to see the lord the prologue. If it be true that good wine needs no bush, 'tis true that a good play needs no epilogue. Yet to good wine they do use good bushes, and good plays prove the better by the help of good epilogues.

What a case am I in, then, that am neither a good epilogue nor cannot insinuate with you in the behalf of a

good play? I am not furnished like a beggar; therefore to
beg will not become me. My way is to conjure you, and I'll
begin with the women: I charge you, O women, to like as
much of this play as please you. And I charge you, O men,
for the love you bear to women—as I perceive by your
simpering, none of you hates them—that between you
and the women, the play may please. If I were a woman
I would kiss as many of you as had beards that pleased
me, complexions that liked me, and breaths that I defied
not. And I am sure, as many as have good beards or good
faces or sweet breaths will for my kind offer, when I make
curtsey, bid me farewell. (5.4.190–207)

Having Rosalind come out for one more turn is a superb choice.
There had been no female character like her on the stage, either in
Shakespeare's plays or those of his contemporary dramatists. This
is an implicit celebration of a signal accomplishment, resembling
Puck's epilogue in its motivation and emphasis.

Rosalind hardly bothers to apologize for the unusual fact of
an epilogue, especially one spoken by a female character. If good
wine needs no bush, she suggests, there is nevertheless no harm in
a little advertising, the bush bringing attention to the wine, and
the epilogue, similarly, making a good play "prove the better." But
she does note the differences between this epilogue and others,
and intrigues us immediately, as is characteristic of her: Rosalind
does not follow fashion, she creates it. She can call attention to
her unusual situation even as she justifies it, refusing to apologize
or beg.

She comes not to beg, but to conjure. She has previously an-
nounced herself as capable of magic, which is the way she seems
to the other characters, not so much to us, who have seen her
arrangements from behind the scenes, as it were. And her conjur-
ing turns out just to be a plea to the ladies to take the initiative

in helping the men recognize and celebrate what she has come to mean.

Gender, then, becomes an issue. Since Rosalind was played by a boy, we can assume that Shakespeare had an extraordinarily gifted young actor, one he felt could handle such an innovative and demanding part. Why not give both the boy and the character the last word, a separate curtain call and, who knows?—perhaps a shower of coins for the confident youngster. The speech teases us with the fact that we have been willing to take the boy as a woman, a woman, moreover, who dresses as a man and then pretends to be acting as a woman in the mock-courtship. We may say that the make-believe world of the pastoral romance has made this possible, but it is not really necessary as an explanation, as Shakespeare had already used the device in two earlier comedies, *The Two Gentlemen of Verona* and *The Merchant of Venice*. Here, though, he takes it further and extracts more comedy from it than in any other play.

Gender becomes less crucial in the process. The point about Rosalind is not so much that she is a disguised woman (played by a boy actor) as that she can test her own readiness for love and marriage along with the readiness of her infatuated suitor. Styles of wooing can be teased and problems of sustaining love can be aired in the safe space of the "play" courtship she sets up. We have an implicit celebration of acting, once more, and a triumph of affirmation of human love in the face of adversity.

The dream of a better world that is the foundation of pastoral is not necessarily endorsed or sustained by the play. The forest of Arden and the exile court of Duke Senior have their share of poverty, starvation, bad weather, bloody hunts, and indifferent landlords. Just as Rosalind is both genders, so is her world both pastoral and anti-pastoral.

The idealism and utopian projection of pastoral need such testing if they are to survive, let alone flourish. So Rosalind, in her epilogue, uses "if," just as it has been used again and again throughout the play, underlining the fact of hypothesis so that we don't get lost in ideals.

"If I were a woman"—this is why the epilogue's main joke won't work in modern productions where an actress plays Rosalind; the joke will disappear. But in the context of Shakespeare's company and audience, it is rich with implication. "If I were a woman I would kiss as many of the men as suited me." The beards, complexions, and breaths in the audience, however, must forego the kissing and provide applause instead, since she is not a woman. Perhaps that's as it should be, both in the playhouse and in private performances. Desire can rear its head in either circumstance. As several commentators have suggested, there is some homoerotic teasing here, but it is good-natured. Rosalind, boy-girl-boy-girl, is an object of admiration and desire, whatever the gender. Everyone can love her, everyone can desire her, a little or a lot.

Appealing to the women in the audience, many of whom were probably already fans of Lodge's romance, Rosalind puts them in charge of the male responses, replicating the authority she has just exercised in the forest, over the plot. The stratagem echoes the gender division that was exploited in Kemp's epilogue to *2 Henry IV*, but it has more bite and more wit in this setting and with this play.

*

The sophistication, both of character and of epilogue, may lead us to speculate about the play's intended audience. It is elegant enough about matters of literary fashion (there are two allusions to Christopher Marlowe in the play and a good deal of attention, via Jaques, to the then-current vogue for satire, along with the multifaceted teasing of pastoral's popularity) to have pleased a courtly or aristocratic audience. That does not mean it was unsuitable for the playhouse, but it does suggest that Shakespeare had an eye for its appeal to the court and to aristocratic patrons for whom the players might perform while on tour.

That would account for the epilogue's suggestion that there are as many ladies in the audience as men, for example (less likely at the Globe). We can imagine the players on the road, like the troupe in *Hamlet*, earning what they can through the patronage of aristocrats and great houses.

In fact, we do know of one performance of this play at a great house, a perfect place for a witty comedy centered on pastoral. Wilton, the seat of the Herbert family, could boast of being the place where Philip Sidney composed his *Arcadia*, a collection of pastoral romances. He wrote it for his sister, the Countess of Pembroke and mother of the man who may have been the subject and object of Shakespeare's sonnets, William Herbert, eventually Earl of Pembroke. No other great house in England, not even Penshurst, could be called such a center of literary excellence and taste, and Mary Sidney, the Countess, herself an accomplished poet, author, and translator, had no rivals as an arbiter of literary judgment and discrimination. That Shakespeare's company would be delighted to perform at Wilton, for that family and their friends, goes without saying. Pleasing the Herberts would prove to them and to others that they were appealing to the most refined and educated tastes, as well as to the playhouse audiences.

The performance of *As You Like It* at Wilton that we know of happened in December 1603, four and a half years after the play was first written and performed. It was revived for King James, who had been hunting in the neighborhood and who was ready to be introduced to the work of Shakespeare's company, which would soon come under his protection and sponsorship as the King's Men. Royal favor would come to mean a great deal if they could charm the somewhat inattentive monarch. As things turned out, the Court and the King favored them greatly; they played before him even more often than they had for Elizabeth. Introducing him to this highly sophisticated and hugely entertaining comedy, in a perfect rural setting, may have helped turn the trick.

So we have the appropriate setting for the play, and the best possible circumstances of audience. While James came to the throne well after *As You Like It* was first performed, he would not have been familiar with it. But it seems likely that the Herbert family already knew it, and even likely that the players had performed it at Wilton at an earlier time. A request for a revival, partly to please the King and partly to revisit a family favorite, seems the most plausible scenario.

My own guess is that Shakespeare's first visit to Wilton happened in April of 1597, when he may have presented the first 17 of the sonnets to William Herbert on the occasion of his 17th birthday. Their theme was one that would please Herbert's parents, who wanted their son to marry and settle down, just as each of those sonnets urged. The Countess may well have commissioned them. If I am right, this would have led to a bond between the playwright (who went on to fall in love with WH) and the family. It is a bond that *As You Like It* might be thought to celebrate and strengthen. That, at any rate, is my sense of the backstory for the 1603 performance. The Herberts knew Shakespeare and he knew them. His 1599 comedy would surely have been one of their favorites among his plays.

In his book about Wilton and the Herberts, *Earls of Paradise*, Adam Nicholson goes further. The version of the play that we have, he argues, is a revision made for that 1603 performance, an attempt not only to please the King but to instruct him in mercy toward Walter Raleigh and some conspirators who were scheduled to be executed in just a few days, at nearby Winchester. Nicholson gives a very persuasive account of the play and its circumstances, and while he does not discuss the epilogue, I suspect he would argue that it was especially composed for this performance. The King was certainly no stranger to homoerotic impulses, so bringing the boy/Rosalind out to tease him and please him seems especially appropriate.

That pleasing and teasing might have happened at earlier performances as well, of course. We have just the Folio text for this play, so there's no way of dating the epilogue to early performances, as we could do had there been a Quarto publication.

As I have argued before, the epilogue can be seen as a liminal space, a transition for the actor and the company between the heightened reality of performance and the ordinary world to which both audience and performers must return. The boy who played Rosalind takes his bow both as the character and as the performer. The risk in this case feels minimal, with the success of the play behind him. The final scene has felt generous and a bit magical. There is a masque that Rosalind has arranged: the appearance of Hymen, god of marriage. Then there is a dance of all the couples (four of them in this case) who are going to be wedded. Then, and only then, Rosalind, who is also now the gifted boy who has played her, steps forward, surprising the audience with his/her saucy speech. It would have been a different boy in 1603, as the original Rosalind's voice would have changed by then. But both in 1599, if we date the epilogue to the original performances, and in 1603, if we take it to be composed for Wilton, we can detect a note of confidence in the playwright's design and choices. The troublesome clown Kemp has been replaced by the new one, Robert Armin, for whom the part of Touchstone has been designed. The company that had been the Lord Chamberlain's Men and would soon become the King's Men both mocked and celebrated pastoral with this play, and the three and a half years between its writing and the Wilton revival had not managed to make it feel dated. Whether Rosalind spoke her epilogue in the public theater, or at a private performance, or

both, she reflected the playwright's confidence in his accomplishment. Unlike the prose epilogues to *2 Henry IV*, this one need not
apologize or defend. Like Puck's epilogue, it underlines the joy of
creation, a creating that is saturated with the recognition that all
the world's a stage and all the men and women "merely players."

4. OUR BENDING AUTHOR

Henry V, 1599

As we have seen, an occasional chorus is not an unusual choice for Shakespeare. Sometimes a chorus may come to speak a prologue, as does Rumor ("painted full of tongues") in *2 Henry IV*, and the armed prologue that introduces *Troilus and Cressida*. We have already examined the Chorus that opens *Romeo and Juliet* and then makes one more appearance, to start the second act. A chorus can even appear without warning in the middle of a play, as does Father Time in *The Winter's Tale*. Only two plays, however, employ a chorus from start to finish: *Pericles* (which we'll treat later) and *Henry V*. Because their choruses comment throughout the action, those two plays have epilogues, and thus belong within the parameters of this study.

We already have developed some context for the *Henry V* chorus and epilogue, having seen the issues that produced two (or three) epilogues for *2 Henry IV*. One of those epilogues already promised a sequel; it would be hard to imagine that Shakespeare would drop the story of Hal's prodigality and eventual kingship without going on to his well known and much admired military triumphs against the French. Shakespeare was undoubtedly committed to completing his second four-play sequence about English monarchy and history. But why would he then decide that this fourth play must have a chorus?

To be sure, the playwright's methods had shifted around considerably as the cycle was being written and performed. The plays formed a sequence, but Shakespeare must also have wanted to avoid repeating himself dramaturgically, so that each installment contained surprising innovations:

- *Richard II* was ceremonial and even ritualistic much of the time, mounting a poetry of loss and compromised ideals to surround a power struggle leading to the abdication and death of a monarch whom some have called the last medieval king.

- The next play, *1 Henry IV*, brought us a very different world, one with Falstaff and the tavern and robbery scenes, along with fascinating characters like Hotspur and Glendower. It was enormously entertaining and innovative, full of elements that earlier history plays by Shakespeare had not anticipated. It told Hal's prodigal son story with confidence and elation.

- Then, in effect, Shakespeare rewrote it, as *2 Henry IV*, this time emphasizing old age, sickness, and a much more realistic sense of social corruption and the costliness of war. It opened, as we know, with an emphatic prologue, spoken by Rumor. And it closed with the various epilogues we have examined, reflecting concern about audience response and reaffirming a commitment to the ongoing four-play sequence. The playwright seemed to feel the need for closing statements that sought to reassure, predict, and apologize for misunderstandings. Where would he go next in dealing with Hal/Henry's success as a warrior monarch?

The Chorus comes out to greet us at the beginning of *Henry V*, to help establish the transition and to set a new tone:

Oh, for a muse of fire that would ascend
The brightest heaven of invention,
A kingdom for a stage, princes to act,
And monarchs to behold the swelling scene.
Then should the warlike Harry, like himself,
Assume the port of Mars, and at his heels,
Leashed in like hounds, should famine, sword, and fire
Crouch for employment. (Pro.1–8)

This strikes an expansive, epic note, responding to what the audience no doubt partly anticipated: the story of a kingship that was considered far more successful than those of Richard II and Henry IV. This warrior-king triumphed over the French and won back English rights and glory, as well as a French princess for his bride. An adequate portrait, we're told at the outset, could be played by princes for an audience of monarchs, and it would compare him to the god of war!

No sooner are we reminded of that time of English triumph, however, than the Chorus introduces complications to such stirring possibilities:

But pardon, gentles all,
The flat unraisèd spirits that hath dared
On this unworthy scaffold to bring forth
So great an object. Can this cockpit hold
The vasty fields of France? Or may we cram
Within this wooden O the very casques
That did affright the air at Agincourt?
Oh, pardon, since a crooked figure may
Attest in little place a million,

And let us, ciphers to this great account,
On your imaginary forces work. (8–18)

This is the ninth history play that Shakespeare and his company have performed in as many years, work that has been enormously popular and successful. Now, suddenly, they feel apologetic and self-conscious? Is their theater (the newly rebuilt Globe on the South Bank) merely a cockpit, a wooden O?

Two explanations may be proposed for this new complication of outlook. The first concerns that epic register envisioned by the opening lines of the Chorus. This material, both heroic and patriotic, is the stuff of epic, and therefore particularly demanding of resonant presentation; it seems to demand a style and opulence the players will have to stretch themselves to provide.

But the other explanation may weigh even more heavily: history plays were slipping out of style, and as the fashion ebbed, the tide of criticism rose. Ben Jonson, in his prologue to *Every Man in His Humour*, mocked plays where the players

With three rusty swords
And help of some few foot-and-half-foot words
Fight over York and Lancaster's long jars,
And in the tiring-house bring wounds to scars.

Such criticism may have made the players wince. How indeed could they hope to do justice to history, and especially to battle scenes that should involve whole armies? More and more, one gathers, people had begun pointing out the shortcomings of the genre. Since entire reigns of kings were covered, there could be no observation of the classical unities of time, place, and action, Jonson's classicist formula, evoked partly as a means of trying to one-up his rival Shakespeare. Moreover, questions of the unities aside, there was simply no way, the argument ran, that great historical events could be adequately presented on the contemporary stage.

If fashion had begun to run against the English chronicle play, Shakespeare could have decided to abandon the genre altogether, as subsequently happened (the very late *Henry VIII* being the one exception). But he had already committed himself to the completion of Hal's coming-of-age story. And as the pre-eminent writer of history plays in his generation, he had a sizable stake in the quarrel, and an accomplishment to defend. He had committed himself to a play about Henry V's triumph as king and general. What better way to disarm audience mutterings about problems of performance and representation than by anticipating and displaying those problems through the mouth of the Chorus?

We might note in passing here that the Quarto version of *Henry V* does not include the Chorus and his speeches. This does not mean, I think, that they were added later, but it does suggest that the play could be cut down for touring and the choruses treated as detachable. Maybe out on the road audiences were less likely to question whether the genre had passed out of fashion, or whether the theater and the players were adequate to the material?

The players are well aware, it turns out, of the problems they face. What they need, even more than usual, is the audience's imaginative cooperation:

> Suppose within the girdle of these walls
> Are now confined two mighty monarchies,
> Whose high, uprearèd, and abutting fronts
> The perilous narrow ocean parts asunder.
> Piece out our imperfections with your thoughts;
> Into a thousand parts divide one man
> And make imaginary puissance. (19–25)

This modest challenge would be difficult to resist. The verse is compelling, and nearly everyone who has come to see the play would rather have it succeed than fail; if the implied contract between players and audience is spelled out for once, what's the harm in that?

> Think, when we talk of horses, that you see them
> Printing their proud hooves i'th' receiving earth.
> For 'tis your thoughts that now must deck our kings,
> Carry them here and there, jumping o'er times,
> Turning th'accomplishment of many years
> Into an hourglass: for the which supply,
> Admit me Chorus to this history,
> Who Prologue-like your humble patience pray,
> Gently to hear, kindly to judge our play. (26–34)

The theatrical self-consciousness that produced plays within plays in earlier dramatic experiments here takes the form of examining how performance necessarily involves creativity on both sides of the footlights. The Chorus, then, speaks partly for the playwright, partly for the players, and partly for the audience, who can make the play a success if they are disposed to collaborate. To identify the Chorus too firmly with Shakespeare would blur the emphasis on this joint venture, a three-way enterprise in which he is simply a partner and participant, or so the argument runs. The rhetoric of the chorus thus resists the ideal of single authorship, as well as any division of interest and opinion among the company and with their audience.

We can see this partly as clever maneuvering on the author's part, but it should also serve to remind us that individual authorship was not as highly valued (Jonson notwithstanding) as in later times. Everything we know about Shakespeare suggests that he saw his dramatic art as collaborative and temporary. We see his creative genius now through hindsight, but we do him an injustice if we think his individuality made him a proud and isolated figure.

It should come as no surprise that the use of a chorus in this play did not mollify Jonson or dispose of his objections. In that same prologue to *Every Man in His Humour* (which belongs not to the 1601 Quarto but to the 1616 Folio) he notes that his is a play "Where neither Chorus wafts you o'er the seas / Nor creaking throne comes down, the boys to please." The second line refers to theophanies like the one in *Cymbeline* where Jupiter comes down "in thunder and lightning, seated upon an eagle," but the first constitutes an attack on *Henry V* as well as *Pericles*, where choruses were used for exactly that purpose.

Jonson simply could not leave these issues alone. Even though *EMI* had been first performed by Shakespeare's company, the sniping continued. One tradition (from Rowe) says that Jonson's play was first going to be turned down by the Chamberlain's Men until Shakespeare interceded and persuaded them to take it (Fraser, 126f.). This showed good taste—it's a deft and witty comedy—as well as personal generosity. But Jonson was on his way to a different definition of authorship. He would write for the children's companies and seek aristocratic patronage. And his definition of the way a career was shaped for a man of letters was the one that prevailed. It simply wasn't Shakespeare's.

Put yourself in Jonson's place: you are a good playwright but you must always suffer comparison to Will Shakespeare, who, while not yet acknowledged as a great dramatist, is impossibly tough competition. You *have* to denigrate him and his art in order to promote yourself and persuade his audience to prefer your offerings.

Now put yourself in Shakespeare's place: you take this man in and promote his work, despite his criticism and carping. This suggests that you can rise above the objections, having a good deal of confidence in yourself and what you do. It also suggests, as I indicated earlier, that you are less personally invested in your authorial accomplishments and much more firmly associated with the welfare and enterprise of your acting company. Their interest and successes are identical with yours and your personal fame doesn't greatly interest you, partly because it could easily get in the way of the joint enterprise of the Chamberlain's Men and partly because you have long since tamed your restless ego.

The Jonson saga goes on, and it does not seem ever to have led to a complete falling out or to significant bitterness. Theirs remained a more or less friendly rivalry, more a preoccupation of Jonson than of Shakespeare. When Jonson parted company with the Lord Chamberlain's Men and attacked them, they responded through their other playwright, Dekker, rather than through Shakespeare. And we know how fine and generous a tribute Jonson composed for Shakespeare when the plays were collected for the First Folio.

Meanwhile, it's clear that Shakespeare was enjoying the task he had assigned himself in composing the lines of the Chorus. They sizzle with eloquence:

> Now all the youth of England are on fire,
> And silken dalliance in the wardrobe lies.
> Now thrive the armorers, and honor's thought
> Reigns solely in the breast of every man.
> They sell the pasture now to buy the horse,
> Following the mirror of all Christian kings
> With wingèd heels, as English Mercuries. (2.0.1–7)

The choruses may sometimes offer to fill in the narrative or offer apology for the difficulty of the material, but they also act to charge our sense of excitement and energy:

Now entertain conjecture of a time
When creeping murmur and the poring dark
Fills the wide vessel of the universe.
From camp to camp, through the foul womb of night,
The hum of either army stilly sounds,
That the fixed sentinels almost receive
The secret whispers of each other's watch.
Fire answers fire, and through their paly flames
Each battle sees the other's umbered face. (4.0.1–9)

Commentators on the play have had two kinds of objection to these dashing and poetic interludes by the Chorus. The dramatist's art is compromised, they argue, when narration replaces dramatization. And they have been disappointed to discover that the choruses do not unequivocally represent the author's view of the story. The first objection reflects Jonson's sense that there must be rules which are observed, rules handed down through the ages. That Shakespeare never felt bound by such rules is manifest and, I have always felt, a matter for celebration.

The second objection is more subtle. As we discover in the play an extremely complicated portrait of its hero and his accomplishments, it's as though we come to feel that the Chorus has tried to mislead us, to "spin" Henry. This king is cold, opportunistic, and manipulative; he orders the French prisoners executed, he dismisses his old comrade Bardolph to be hanged without a trace of regret, and he is unwilling to acknowledge any guilt he may incur by leading men to their deaths. He may be a capable ruler and a brave soldier, but the play gives us plenty of opportunities to see him more as a politician and even a demagogue than the Chorus would seem to want to consider or mention.

Again, this seems to me not a shortcoming but a strength, allowing us to see the historical events from many angles. The Chorus, thrilled by the epic sweep and the poetry of war, provides one of them. Expecting him to have the more disillusioned insights would be inconsistent. That truly would constitute an undermining of dramatic possibility. The Chorus could celebrate this material and this hero, and enlist the audience's cooperation with the production, but he could not become a detractor of the King.

Thus it is that the Chorus eventually feels somewhat less relevant. As our knowledge grows and our perspective complicates, his authority gradually recedes. When he is singing his epic theme, he is confident and persuasive. When he is having to manage the dramatic action and supervise more mundane matters—where we are now, where we will be next—he is far less impressive. The Chorus' speech before the fifth act feels more strained and cobbled together than the earlier ones. It glances at the Earl of Essex and his Irish campaign, expressing a hope for success that would be similar to "this Harry." (The campaign would turn out to be disastrous.) And it concludes with some remarkably clumsy stagecraft:

> ... and omit
> All the occurrences, whatever chanced,
> Till Harry's back return again to France.
> There we must bring him; and myself have played
> The interim, by remembering you 'tis past.
> Then brook abridgment and your eyes advance
> After your thoughts, straight back again to France. (5.0.40–46)

It may well be that the playwright's inspiration was flagging by the time that he got to this part of the play. But we still have the wooing of Katherine ahead, a scene that plays very well in performance. It seems more likely that Shakespeare, having little further need of the Chorus, is steadily diminishing his role and his effectiveness.

We come now to the sonnet that constitutes the Chorus' last speech and thus, of course, the play's epilogue, our essential subject. It is an attempt, I think, to cover all the bases:

Thus far, with rough and all-unable pen,
Our bending author hath pursued the story,
In little room confining mighty men,
Mangling by starts the full course of their glory.
Small time, but in that small most greatly lived
This star of England. Fortune made his sword,
By which the world's best garden he achieved,
And of it left his son imperial lord.
Henry the Sixth, in infant bands crowned King
Of France and England, did this king succeed,
Whose state so many had the managing
That they lost France and made his England bleed,
Which oft our stage hath shown—and for their sake,
In your fair minds let this acceptance take. (Ep.1–14)

Any conjectures that Shakespeare himself played the Chorus or wanted us to identify him with its point of view are surely dissolved here. He is apologizing, to be sure, through the mouth of the Chorus, but author and chorus are not the same individual. "Our bending author" (who may remind us of the kneeling Shakespeare who could have spoken that court epilogue to *2 Henry IV*), is one of the collaborators who put this all together. Shakespeare has done some mangling, the Chorus admits, while he still retains full admiration for their subject, "This star of England." Chorus is not the author, but he gazes back wistfully toward "the world's best garden" before turning to acknowledge what happened to it, a mangling on a far greater scale, and one which the players have, over time, faithfully portrayed.

Bending and mangling! So the heroism of Henry is tempered once and for all by the recognition that it was followed by mismanagement and civil war. That isn't the players' fault. Their stage has shown the good and the bad. But the bending author may be sending us a reminder and a signal: he, after all, has just completed a sequence of eight history plays, linking the end of a giant circle with its beginning, surveying a cycle that reflects the good and bad of history on a scale and with a determination that we may justly admire and applaud. The eight plays together make more of an epic than any single drama could. If the brightest heaven of invention is accessed, so is the sordid story of civil conflict, murder, unrest, and dissolution.

The connected cycle of kingships certainly made Shakespeare's reputation as a playwright and brought prosperity to his "cry of players." Now it was completed, and the actors would turn to other genres and other themes. "In your fair minds," audience, he suggests, you may well accept such an accomplishment. But it will not be trumpeted and underlined in the manner of Ben Jonson. It will be offered with the humility and circumspection we have come to expect.

5. THE CHANCE OF WAR

Troilus and Cressida, 1602

We come now to a much trickier play and a difficult set of questions, leading to a very strange epilogue. From one perspective, *Troilus and Cressida* is a considerable mess of a play, a chaotic skid across several genres, not to mention tones and attitudes. It seems to fall apart as it comes to a close, resolving very little and frustrating both audience and character expectations—about love, about war, about honor, and, given its magnificent sources, about great literature.

From another angle, however, it might be contended that this is Shakespeare's most characteristic play, a striking reflection of his tendency to experiment with breaking rules and his notorious stretching of boundaries. *Troilus and Cressida* certainly partakes of tragedy, comedy, and history, not to mention satire and burlesque. And generations of scholars have argued about its provenance, seeing it on the one hand as a highly specialized treat for a coterie audience, such as the lawyers and students at the Inns of Court, or on the other as a public playhouse response to the vogue for satire and the war of the theaters, a measured response to the cynical and sophisticated plays being written by Jonson and Marston and Middleton for the children's companies. When it was printed in a 1609 quarto, it was accompanied by an advertisement that claimed it had not been performed publicly and was indeed caviar to the general, too learned and witty to succeed in the popular theater. Since such characterizations are rarities in Shakespeare's case, the claim deserves to be taken seriously. And since the play is certainly much enhanced if audiences are familiar with the *Iliad* and with Chaucer's telling of the Troilus and Cressida story, because it gives a relatively savage treatment to both of those classic texts, it can certainly be said to be aimed at an educated and well-read elite.

At the same time, as we will see, the epilogue strongly suggests a public performance and a playhouse audience. So once again we are faced with tendencies that seem to be characteristic of this playwright: that he could write with one eye on performance at the Globe and the other on what private audiences might like and find especially suited to them and their circumstances. The tendency begins as early as *The Comedy of Errors* and continues right on through the canon. Here it reaches what may be its limit, a play so divided against itself or so fully in touch with contrary possibilities that it falls between its two targets and quite possibly pleases neither. Still, knowing how deft Shakespeare was by this time in his career, we can also imagine it pleasing both kinds of audience and going on to test us and our capabilities instead.

Eyeing two different kinds of audience could also mean different versions for different venues, of course, but the practice can be seen as habitual, the technique of an artist with a shrewd business sense. When he could write something like *Macbeth*, directly addressing the King's fascination with witches and obsession with his Scottish lineage and at the same time producing a riveting tragedy for the popular theater, Shakespeare may have been at his happiest. He seems to have enjoyed rising to the challenge.

There are always possibilities of revision lurking around such shifts in performance circumstance. As suggested earlier, the single version of *As You Like It* we have, including its epilogue, may have been specifically crafted for presentation at Wilton House. And similar questions surround *A Midsummer Night's Dream*, with respect to the aristocratic celebration of a marriage. As for *Troilus and Cressida*, it's certainly likely that the advertisement's claim that the play was "a new play, never staled with the stage, never clapper-clawed with the palms of the vulgar" was based, at least in part, on the fact of revision. We have no way of recovering an original version.

Shakespeare is in an unusual frame of mind here, but he is remarkably consistent. This play was performed, then shelved, then revived for publication because it may have had a kind of underground reputation. People wanted to read it because of its notoriety. Being packed with incidents and characters that constitute a kind of running commentary on, and revision of, Homer and Chaucer, it is a masterpiece of its kind, but still one of the strangest plays in the Shakespearean canon. And its epilogue, as we will see, punches that strangeness home.

What we have throughout is a text that seems fairly determined to be confrontational. The first notes are struck in the Prologue:

In Troy, there lies the scene. From isles of Greece
The princes orgulous, their high blood chafed,
Have to the port of Athens sent their ships,
Fraught with the ministers and instruments
Of cruel war. Sixty and nine that wore
Their crownets regal from th'Athenian bay
Put forth toward Phrygia, and their vow is made
To ransack Troy, within whose strong immures
The ravished Helen, Menelaus' queen,
With wanton Paris sleeps—and that's the quarrel. (Pro.1–10)

The diction is splendid, but it also feels inflated, overdone. The comparison to the opening chorus to *Henry V* is instructive. In both cases we are stirred by epic images, but in this instance we are also brought to a reductive point: "and that's the quarrel." It's all about a "ravished" queen who seems to have adapted (anticipating Cressida) to her new bed and lover.

> To Tenedos they come,
> And the deep-drawing barks do there disgorge
> Their warlike freightage. Now on Dardan plains
> The fresh and yet unbruisèd Greeks do pitch
> Their brave pavilions. Priam's six-gated city—
> Dardan, and Timbria, Helias, Chetas, Troien,
> And Antenorides—with massive staples
> And corresponsive and fulfilling bolts
> Spar up the sons of Troy. (11–19)

Again, we have a mixture of the heroic and the ridiculous, naming each of the gates and describing their bolts as "corresponsive and fulfilling." It is wonderful blank verse, but it has an odor of deliberate fustian about it, as if first looking into Chapman's Homer has impressed this author less than it would Keats two centuries later.

Time now for the prologue to get to the point:

> Now expectation, tickling skittish spirits
> On one and other side, Trojan and Greek,
> Sets all on hazard. And hither am I come,
> A Prologue armed, but not in confidence
> Of author's pen or actor's voice, but suited
> In like conditions as our argument,
> To tell you, fair beholders, that our play
> Leaps o'er the vaunt and firstlings of those broils,

Beginning in the middle, starting thence away
To what may be digested in a play.
Like or find fault, do as your pleasures are,
Now good or bad, 'tis but the chance of war. (20–31)

That the prologue is armed is of course convenient, as he is going
to portray a soldier shortly, Trojan or Greek. It is also a jab at
Jonson, who had used an armed prologue in his play *Poetaster*, in
1601, as a way to be confrontational with his audience, supposedly driving off Envy. This armed presenter is not displaying such
confidence or belligerence, but is simply dressed appropriately for
the occasion. He wants the audience to know that, like an epic
poem, the play begins *in medias res*, and is hence respectable in its
literary grounding. His ironic handling of his language and attitude climaxes in the couplet, expressing indifference, as opposed
to the more normal cajoling of favor ("we hope you like it, we aim
to please," etc.), and leaving all judgment to the audience and "the
chance of war." We seem to be entering a world where unpredict-
ability rules, both with warriors and with lovers, and given that,
the players are supposedly somewhat indifferent to our response.
If what we see strikes us as bad, we are reacting more to the reality
of war than to the problematics of players and their theater.

It is risky to tell an audience to consult their own tastes and
pleasures, but we are talking about a playwright who has used
titles like *As You Like It* and *What You Will* to admit that he is at
least guardedly responsive to popularity and taste, a responsive-
ness that leads eventually to *Pericles* but arrives there by way of
plays like this one. Tastes shift, fashions alter. The players aim to
please, but they also have their own integrity to think about. The
audience needs to respect that.

To me this prologue feels unlike a later revision, and more like
a public playhouse announcement at an early performance, close
enough in time to *Poetaster* to associate the play with the war of

the theaters where Marston, Jonson, Dekker, and Shakespeare were all taking potshots at one another. It is a masterly, if unsettling, beginning. It sounds a tone that is distinct from any other Shakespeare play we know.

From that opening the play moves forward to cover both the story of the *Iliad* and the spoiled romance of Chaucer's ill-fated lovers. Two literary masterpieces are going to get a rough and somewhat summary treatment. None of the characters manage to live up to their stated ideals or to their codes of martial honor and courtly love. Ulysses is the central intelligence, but he is clever and manipulative rather than honorable and heroic. As the play progresses toward its end, the nasty Thersites, acting as a prowling chorus, can point out to us that it's all "Lechery, lechery, still wars and lechery, nothing else holds fashion." He has watched Troilus watching Cressida betray him, and he will appear regularly in the final battle scenes to characterize their brutality and meaninglessness.

Given Thersites' harsh choric role, we might well expect him to speak the epilogue, but instead it is Pandarus, Cressida's lecherous uncle, who is left at last on stage to turn his attention to the audience. He has engineered the union of Troilus and Cressida with a florid and obsessive dwelling on sex, but is now rejected by Troilus and is suddenly feeling his age and illness, presumably from venereal disease. Troilus has harshly repudiated him, so that he has abruptly joined the category Thersites inhabits, that of disgusting and disgusted witness. In the first part of his epilogue his self-pity leads him to address his counterparts in the audience:

A goodly medicine for my aching bones. Oh, world, world, world! Thus is the poor agent despised. O traitors and bawds, how earnestly are you set a-work, and how ill requited. Why should our endeavor be so desired and the

performance so loathed? What verse for it? What instance
for it? Let me see,

>Full merrily the humble-bee doth sing
>Till he hath lost his honey and his sting;
>And, being once subdued in armèd tail,
>Sweet honey and sweet notes together fail. (5.11.35–44)

The little verse compounds the lovers, who are urgent until con-
summation and disaffected or disgusted afterwards, with those
who serve their desires, sought eagerly for their services and then
repudiated for trafficking in flesh and lust. Pandarus is the origin
and archetype of something so familiar to the audience at the
Globe that they cannot continue to pretend a comfortable distance from this classical and medieval story. This is the very world
they live in, here and now on the South Bank of the Thames,
where prostitution flourishes and venereal disease abounds.

The prevalence of disease, now taking its rapid toll on
Pandarus, underlines the disgust that concupiscence seems to have
invoked for Shakespeare. He treats the brothel world in several
plays, sometimes with a rough affection, as with Doll Tearsheet
in *2 Henry IV* and Pompey Bum in *Measure for Measure*, but also
with disgust, as in *Pericles*. In that play Marina, confronting the
bawd Bolt, echoes what the Duke in *Measure for Measure* had said
to Pompey about making a living from lust:

>Thou art the damnèd doorkeeper to every
>Coistrel that comes inquiring for his Tib.
>To the choleric fisting of every rogue
>Thy ear is liable; thy food is such
>As hath been belched on by infected lungs. (4.6.150–54)

Here, now, in London, in the first few years of the seventeenth
century, it is no longer the matter of Troy, the once-respectable

material of Homer and Chaucer. It is the Globe audience with its
considerable share of prostitutes, customers, and pimps. Pandarus
continues:

> Good traders in the flesh, set this in your painted cloths:
> As many as be here of panders' hall,
> Your eyes, half out, weep out at Pandar's fall.
> Or if you cannot weep, yet give some groans,
> Though not for me, yet for your aching bones.
> Brethren and sisters of the hold-door trade,
> Some two months hence my will shall here be made.
> It should be now, but that my fear is this:
> Some gallèd goose of Winchester would hiss.
> Till then I'll sweat and seek about for eases,
> And at that time bequeath you my diseases. (5.11.45–55)

It's as though Pandarus's last hope in life and history is for some
consideration from the guild of pimps and prostitutes whose
emblem he has become. He appeals to them for a sympathy he
knows they probably cannot summon. If they can't weep for him,
they can groan for their own disease-ridden bodies. He won't bequeath them his diseases now, lest he get hissed at by some local
whore (after this remark, no one is likely to be willing to hiss).
But he will bequeath (and die?) in two months and will mingle
among them until then, trying the sweating cure and various
painkillers, but like them fated to perish through his association
with flesh-peddling.

It is a devastating close to the play, bringing the action quite
suddenly into the sordid present and collapsing the great time in-
terval between the first Pandar and all the contemporary panders
plying their trade around the Bankside. It also makes this actor a
pandering go-between from players to audience, reducing the theater to another sort of flesh-peddling, perhaps pimping bad plays

to poor tastes. It must have brought everybody up short, and in that sense it is not merely a teasing or tweaking, as with Puck's epilogue, but something nastier and more uncompromising. What's liminal here is not so much the transition from character to actor as from ancient archetype to its most familiar and contemporary embodiment. The actor playing Pandarus plays at becoming a contemporary London pimp.

In that respect the epilogue is of a piece with the rest of the play, from the prologue on. Once embarked on the debunking of military prowess and romantic love, as represented by two great writers, Shakespeare is true to his choice. As I said earlier, this is not typical, but it is remarkably consistent, right to this final, devastating moment. Pandarus speaks for the play as a whole, for its author and players and audience, all complicit in a nasty mix of cheapened sex and distortive violence.

6. A Beggar King

All's Well That Ends Well, 1604

This play belongs to a period when Shakespeare was mainly writing tragedies, and when his comedies were "problematic," i.e., testing and stretching the genre he had so successfully mastered in plays like *A Midsummer Night's Dream*, *Much Ado About Nothing*, *As You Like It*, and *Twelfth Night*. Along with *Measure for Measure* and *Troilus and Cressida* (some would add the earlier comedy, *The Merchant of Venice*), *All's Well* can be seen as a revisiting of the genre with an intention to test its limits and meanings. This play can also be linked to the late romances, working as it does with folktale material and moving toward an ending which is clearly a "storybook" close rather than a character-driven and realistic one. We can say that comic happy endings are always conventional rather than realistic, but the late comedies and then the romances that follow force that awareness on us in unprecedented ways. As we talk about their happy endings, we feel the need to put "happy" in quotes. Yes, they are happy, but never unqualifiedly so, never without questions and problems.

In recent years stage productions that have taken this play's text at face value (rather than apologizing for its supposed shortcomings) have shown it to be one of the most moving and fascinating plays in the Shakespearean canon. If it is, as some have suggested, the *Love's Labour's Won* that we know existed by 1598, it is most certainly a much-revised version of that play, rewritten to align with the darker thinking and deliberate risk-taking of Shakespeare's later years.

The risk-taking in this play consists of using a very simple, even primitive story and treating it as real, with fully rounded and believable characters acting out its folktale pattern. Helena wins her husband by fulfilling his impossible demand: to be with child by him and to possess the heirloom ring that never leaves his finger. Like patient Griselda, in Chaucer's famous tale, her success allows her to vault from a low-born status to an aristocratic title (she will be Countess of Rousillon), in an unlikely leap. It is a wish-fulfillment tale, like the more familiar Cinderella story, and it's as if Shakespeare asked himself whether it could be brought off in a realistic and sophisticated treatment, giving the audience a double consciousness: aware of the unlikeliness of the tale yet fascinated by its realization in the form of believable people and circumstances. From the title on, the play asks us to interest ourselves in this challenge. Can we still like the folktale when it is fleshed out, and can we, especially, assent to its ending, knowing Helena and Bertram as we do? Bertram is odious and deceitful, Helena is the victim of her own passion for him, and the more likeable older generation, fond of her and appalled by him, are unable to make things right, try as they might.

A considerable tension, therefore, surrounds the climax of the play as it moves toward Helena's success, Bertram's exposure and humiliation, and the revelation of how it has all come about. The King of France has been instrumental to the story. His wasting illness, a fistula cured by Helena (who is the daughter of a famous physician), has led him to promise her any of his courtiers in marriage as a reward. Having long nursed a secret passion for Bertram, she chooses him. Once he refuses her, and is forced by the King to accept and marry her, the folktale plot is set in motion. We may be engrossed enough in the story and characters to accept it, but we are bound to question it sooner or later.

We are constantly being headed away from simplistic judgments about good and bad, right and wrong. Parolles, Bertram's disgraceful companion, could become a scapegoat who, having led him astray, is justly exposed as a coward and a liar, allowing Bertram an opportunity to reform. But it doesn't work that way. Parolles' humanity—"Simply the thing I am / Shall make me live"—asserts itself and, if it doesn't endear him to us, at least allows us pity and sympathy. Bertram, meanwhile, a sort of failed prodigal son, does not absorb the lesson that his friend, one of the Dumaine brothers, articulates so deftly for us:

> The web of our life is of a mingled yarn, good and ill together: our virtues would be proud if our faults whipped them not, and our crimes would despair if they were not cherished by our virtues. (4.3.70–73)

Given this relativity of judgment, it's not surprising, then, that the phrase of the title, hopeful but sketchy, is reiterated in the last act. The King, as the play closes, is the predictable authority figure who offers the typical comedic summary. He has a concluding speech to the assembled characters, ten lines, five couplets, and in it we seem to have arrived at a satisfactory, though somewhat ambiguous, conclusion:

> Let us from point to point this story know
> To make the even truth in pleasure flow.
> [*To Diana*] If thou beest yet a fresh uncroppèd flower,
> Choose thou thy husband and I'll pay thy dower.
> For I can guess that by thy honest aid
> Thou kep'st a wife herself, thyself a maid.
> Of that and all the progress more and less

Resolvedly more leisure shall express.
All yet seems well, and if it end so meet,
The bitter passed, more welcome is the sweet. (5.3.318–27)

It feels right to have the play's authority figure accepting the strange outcome. Bertram has given Helena the impossible task of obtaining his heirloom ring and becoming pregnant with his child. She has returned from apparent death, having used what we call a bed-trick to prove that his conditions are fulfilled. On the level of folktale, all *is* well. The impossible has been miraculously accomplished; our heroine gets to rise to a new level of class and status and marry the man she loves. Diana, who has helped her, is to be similarly rewarded: the offer to let her choose a husband often draws a knowing laugh; given what's happened with Bertram and Helena, the audience may anticipate a repeat of all the complications, as if the King has learned nothing from these events.

So we recognize the plot completion and the "inevitability" of its outcome. But these characters are sophisticated contemporaries, and it isn't easy to imagine a happy marriage between the Bertram we have come to know and the determined, unhappy Helena who loves him despite his failings. The play's title, and its reiteration by Helena as she is trying to complete her machinations ("All's well that ends well yet, / Though time seem so adverse and means unfit" [5.1.25–26]), is echoed once again by the King: "All yet seems well." This emphasis, surely, with seeming substituted for being, is meant to acknowledge just how problematic this happy ending really is. There's lots of bitter to go with the sweet. The plot has its way, inevitably, but it does not dispose of all the questions it has raised. We are left unsure of how we should feel. A similar disquiet arises at the close of *Measure for Measure*, a companion "problem comedy," where the Duke's sudden and unlooked-for proposal to Isabella leaves us wondering if she will accept him and then manage to be happy with him. There can be no question that by this point in his career, Shakespeare enjoyed problematizing genre and questioning comic plot resolutions, a practice that would very soon lead him into his last phase, the late romances.

The King has certainly been part of all this questionable behavior inside the conventional plot. Helena has cured him of a wasting illness and he has rewarded her by letting her choose a husband. When it becomes clear that Bertram won't cooperate and Helena, deeply embarrassed, asks to have the matter dropped, the King is unable to do the sensible thing and walk away: "My honor's at the stake, which to defeat / I must produce my power. Here, take her hand" (2.3.147–48). He's a king, after all, so we understand his behavior even as we realize it would be better to let things take a different course. We take it for granted that a king can and will do as he pleases, even if his choices may prove disastrous. This perception, I think, is what brings us the epilogue: six more lines, three couplets, as the King steps forward, probably kneels (the posture of supplication that was associated with many epilogues of the period) and addresses the audience:

The King's a beggar now the play is done.
All is well ended if this suit be won,
That you express content, which we will pay
With strife to please you, day exceeding day.
Ours be your patience, then, and yours our parts;
Your gentle hands lend us, and take our hearts. (5.3.328–33)

The collapse of all that authority and power is, of course, based on the recognition of fiction and playing. This king is really an actor, and he and his company are at the mercy of their audience. The players are once again in a liminal circumstance as they suddenly transfer all authority to their spectators. They must wait to see how the play is accepted. Of course the ending was a matter of "seem" rather than "is," given the fact that all playing is illusory.

In asking for applause, "that you express content," the actor/king is acknowledging two role reversals, from king to beggar and from player to audience. "Ours be your patience," he says, referring to their quiet attention to the drama that has just concluded, "and yours our parts." In other words, you will perform now (by applauding, we hope), and we will attend you as you have been attending us. We will trade hands for hearts, a bargain. Our relationship is more mutual and reciprocal than you may realize. You are kings too, and we are beggars.

Perhaps the King can say this because, for all his power and authority, he has had to depend on Helena twice, once for the cure of his illness and again at the end for the untangling of all the riddles of the plot. The very nature of the story has acted as a questioning of his power, not to mention his wisdom and restraint. We like the King, but we finish the story with a strong awareness of his limitations.

The brevity and simplicity of this epilogue, very Shakespearean characteristics, also tend to mask its revolutionary sensibility. The player as beggar, an ambiguous social being then and now, is not that surprising. As more than one critic has noted, players could be thought of as beggars, especially in their dependency on aristocratic and court patronage. Their ambiguous social position was never far from Shakespeare's keen awareness. But this speech also stems from a deep consideration of art's relation to its audience, and it clarifies an aesthetic truth, which is that art exists only in its cooperation and completion by the perceiver or spectator. Inside the story, meaning may seem self-generated and self-contained, but the minute we step outside that story we begin to gather insights about our peculiar relation to it. An interdependency prevails. In this case, in a neat twist, the epilogue transfers the question of what is or isn't "well ended" to the measured judgment of the spectators, and by turning the king's power inside out, so to speak, it reminds us that all power is transitory, even illusory, like the play itself. This anticipates a fuller recognition of the same kind in Prospero's epilogue to *The Tempest*.

Readers may find themselves wondering whether Shakespeare could have played the part of the King, which would allow him, in this case, to speak his own epilogue to his own play. In a way it doesn't matter who spoke the King's epilogue. Whoever does it speaks for the author, but also for the company and for the deepest meanings of the art of playing, "dressed," as Isabella puts it in *Measure for Measure*, "in a little brief authority." That authority, signified by the equivocal King, lasts for the duration of the play, and then it dissolves, like everything else.

7. To Hear an Old Man Sing

Pericles, 1608

We come now to one of the most peculiar plays in the canon. On the one hand, *Pericles* is recognized as the first of the late romances, setting the course for one of the most distinctive shifts of emphasis in all of Shakespeare. On the other hand, it is despised and dismissed by many readers and commentators as a collaboration, with a corrupt text that can never take its place among Shakespeare's major achievements. Recent scholarship has argued that a man named George Wilkins is mainly responsible for the first two acts and that Shakespeare wrote parts, or all, of the rest. Meanwhile, the play has enjoyed some extremely successful productions in recent years, and their power to move audiences and to produce a theatrical experience that feels consistent, purposeful, and distinctive has further complicated the picture.

If we go back to *All's Well* for a moment, we can recall that the task that Shakespeare set himself in that play was that of combining primitive folktale material with fully realized characters and contemporary settings. In this play he has simply jettisoned that challenge and put the folktale material more prominently forward, allowing us to enter a more consistent, if also more quaint and unfashionable, dramatic world. He accomplishes this by having a chorus, and that chorus is a medieval poet, John Gower, a

contemporary of Chaucer, who told the tale of Apollonius of Tyre
(here renamed Pericles) in the old-fashioned genre of metrical
romance.

The choice of Gower as presenter and chorus has to have been
Shakespeare's, in my view. What better way to make him evident
as the quaint old storyteller that he is than to resurrect him from
his tomb in the nearby church of Saint Saviour's and bring him to
the stage of the Globe to introduce, and validate, his tale? Hence
this opening chorus:

> To sing a song that old was sung,
> From ashes ancient Gower is come,
> Assuming man's infirmities
> To glad your ear and please your eyes.
> It hath been sung at festivals,
> On ember eves and holy ales,
> And lords and ladies in their lives
> Have read it for restoratives.
> The purchase is to make men glorious,
> *Et bonum quo antiquius, eo melius.*
> If you, born in these latter times
> When wit's more ripe, accept my rhymes,
> And that to hear an old man sing
> May to your wishes pleasure bring,
> I life would wish, and that I might
> Waste it for you like taper light. (Pro.1–16)

You have had fair warning. You are going to see and hear an
old-fashioned story, told by an old-fashioned poet. If that's not
something you can stomach (meaning you, Ben Jonson), better
leave now.

But it will turn out that people do like such stories, told without apology or transformation. As Gower points out, would the

story have survived so long and been through so many retellings if it lacked real value? Its antiquity brings it back to life, just as he has come out of the grave, a phoenix, burning like a candle, giving heat and light in the cold and darkness. Yes, wit's more ripe, but everyone grew up on stories like this, told around the winter hearth by grandmothers. *Pericles* will become one of Shakespeare's most popular plays.

Having Gower introduce and manage the story, acting as chorus, guarantees that we won't forget that the material is old-fashioned, both quaint and venerable. And Gower's lack of experience in the theater may account for most or all of the dramatic clumsiness we encounter in those first two acts. If Shakespeare had another collaborator, we must not lose sight of the fact that Gower is very evidently his co-author. Productions that muffle or disperse or dispense with the choruses jeopardize their own success. In later romances, like *The Winter's Tale*, whose very title invokes the idea of staging folktales, Shakespeare will not feel the need to underline the quaintness so emphatically. Here, though, he finds a means to examine the value of romances and folktales of this kind without having to mediate the materials as he did in earlier transformations of romance like *All's Well* and, for that matter, *King Lear*.

After a lifetime of experiment in several genres, he seemed disposed to invent, or reinvent, a new one. He had become intensely interested in the relation between the romance, the popular form of narrative fiction that could be subdivided into categories like chivalric and pastoral, and what we now call the folktale, the long tradition of oral storytelling. Interest in romance and its elements had always played a part in his work, especially in the comedies, which draw, as we saw in the case of *As You Like It* and Lodge's *Rosalind*, on the popularity of prose romances among Renaissance writers and readers. But the late plays are romances with a difference. They invoke the tragicomic and fairy-tale spirit of the tradition in a new way, stressing the oral and folk dimension and celebrating innocence, wonder, miracle, and magic.

In considering this renewal of a genre we need to think back to Hellenistic romances, which had some literary standing because they were from the classical world, along with the chivalric and pastoral romances that had great popularity in the middle ages and the Renaissance. But we also need to see their link to the tales that generations of storytellers, especially women, passed down in an oral tradition and told around the fire. What Peele had called an "old wives' tale" and Shakespeare would call *A Winter's Tale* honored these storytellers and the season when rural storytelling especially flourished.

This was not so much a case of reinvigorating a genre passing out of fashion, as with *Henry V*, as it was a deliberate reviving of the dormant fashion for romance from the days of Sir Phillip Sidney, Edmund Spenser, and Shakespeare's early rival and detractor Robert Greene. There had also been some notably clumsy examples of staged romances in the 1580s, when Shakespeare was just starting out as a playwright and actor. Lyly, Peele, and Greene, for example, had all tried their hands at staged romance, the latter two in the popular theaters, Lyly more for a coterie audience. Meanwhile, Sidney's commitment to the classical unities of time, place, and action in drama meant that while he could write and approve of prose romances, he could not bring himself to sanction their performance in the theater. They extended time, varied place, and multiplied action. Sidney makes fun of this in his *Defence of Poesy* without appearing to understand the problem fully. For him, prose romance was fine, staged romance was ridiculous.

That can be seen as exactly the sort of challenge that might tempt a virtuoso and veteran playwright. A revival of romance in the theatrical medium ought to confront the problem of episodic narration head-on. Accompanying this commitment came a determination on Shakespeare's part not to sophisticate or update plots and characters to the extent that he had managed in earlier treatments of romance, like *Twelfth Night* and *All's Well*. Instead of subsuming narrative into drama, and modernizing the sense of the miraculous, Shakespeare became intent on featuring or recapturing the old romances' folktale charm and naiveté. It's as if he wanted his audience not only to *remember* how they responded as children to the folktales they heard around the winter fire but to *re-enter* that sense of wonder all over again, in the presence of mystery and miracle.

In light of that impulse, which we may or may not approve of, the decision to employ a chorus in *Pericles* makes wonderful sense. Shakespeare needed a frame for the story, like the one Peele had used in *The Old Wives' Tale* (ca. 1588), where we see the storyteller at her craft before the actors enter and take over for her. And a storyteller from the past, a contemporary of Chaucer and Langland, the poet John Gower, is an inspired choice. He had retold this old Greek story in his *Confessio Amantis*, a long poem in English, and his tomb was nearby the theater, there on the South Bank. Gower combines literary respectability with a naiveté of language and outlook. No one but Shakespeare would have had the ingenious idea of resurrecting him from his grave to walk over to the stage of the Globe and present a venerable tale. He is like a phoenix, risen from its ashes in a miraculous rebirth (a legend that interested Shakespeare greatly, as his poem "The Phoenix and Turtle" confirms). Because Gower has come to tell a tale that also involves the miraculous resurrections of Marina and Thaisa, his sense of his story's value is firm and specific. The story acquires additional value from its communal and holiday retellings. That aristocrats have valued it, seeing it as spiritually medicinal, helps too.

Gower is also aware that a contemporary audience might worry about their difference from this man and his quaint, even innocent world. That sense of his role certainly acts to charm his audience; his sacrifice and dedication are for our benefit. From two centuries earlier, he brings us a tale many more centuries old. If we feel any veneration for the past, how can we not assent to hear his story? And how could anyone not recognize this gesture as Shakespeare's idea?

Thus, as I have argued elsewhere, we do best to see Shakespeare and Gower as co-authors and collaborators. Shakespeare, characteristically, will remain behind the scenes, while Gower, out front, does his clumsy best to adapt an episodic, tragicomic tale to the contemporary stage. It's a fiction, of course, but an exceptionally interesting and persuasive one.

Gower's choruses are always in character: he is serious about the value of his tale, apt to moralize, and ready to help clarify transitions. He's not a terribly good poet, but that is part of the point, germane to Shakespeare's overall strategy. The mask seldom slips, though when Shakespearean eloquence tends to shine through, it's almost as though we watch Shakespeare remembering to rein himself in:

> Now sleep y-slackèd hath the rouse:
> No din but snores about the house,
> Made louder by the o'erfed breast
> Of this most pompous marriage feast.
> The cat with eyne of burning coal
> Now couches fore the mouse's hole;
> And crickets sing at the oven's mouth
> Are the blither for their drouth.
> Hymen hath brought the bride to bed,
> Where by the loss of maidenhead
> A babe is molded. Be attent,
> And time that is so briefly spent
> With your fine fancies quaintly eche.

What's dumb in show, I'll plain with speech.
  [*Dumbshow*] (3.0.1–14)

The first eight lines are unmistakably Shakespeare's voice and sensibility, reminiscent of the close of *A Midsummer Night's Dream*. But Gower must prevail—this is his story and his show—so we descend to a clumsy dumb-show, and the rest of the chorus, sixty lines in total with the dumb-show in the middle, does not feel very Shakespearean at all.

That does not necessarily mean, as many have argued, that someone else wrote it. More likely it means that Shakespeare is intent on keeping Gower's character and choric style consistently before us. In a similar fashion, as the act goes on to a storm scene, we will hear an eloquence comparable to *King Lear* before the play remembers to settle back into its more medieval and prosaic mode. Part of the fun of *Pericles* lies in watching Shakespeare deliberately repressing his own gifts as a poet in order to keep Gower before us as the stage manager and storyteller most likely to choose this subject, this structure, and this style. The Chorus in *Henry V* was a representative of the company, complicit with them in solving the problem of how to stage difficult material. But Gower is an amateur as a playwright, not to mention someone from the deep past, unfamiliar with modern ways. That can account for some, though perhaps not all, of the dramatic clumsiness that has made commentators argue that Shakespeare had a collaborator in this play. It is almost despite the limitations of Gower's outlook that we get scenes as realistic as those set in the whorehouse, or as effective as the reviving of Thaisa by Cerimon, or as deeply moving as the recognition between Pericles and Marina. A trick has been played on us whereby we assent to the idea of Gower's authorship and outlook only to have Shakespeare, once more, work his inimitable theatrical magic. Then too, the tale belongs, as Gower has told us, to no one author or teller. Its communality is part of its value.

And now we come to the epilogue. We've seen the reunion of Thaisa with her husband and daughter. The rest of the cast has exited, to the typical promise of hearing the whole story told and celebrating the nuptials and reunion. The play could end there, but Shakespeare clearly felt that his debt to Gower, for the story and its episodic but curiously successful staging, needed to be fully paid. So the old poet appears for one last time:

> In Antiochus and his daughter you have heard
> Of monstrous lust the due and just reward;
> In Pericles, his queen, and daughter seen,
> Although assailed with fortune fierce and keen,
> Virtue preserved from fell destruction's blast,
> Led on by heaven and crowned with joy at last.
> In Helicanus may you well descry
> A figure of truth, of faith, of loyalty.
> In reverend Cerimon there well appears
> The worth that learnèd charity aye wears.
> For wicked Cleon and his wife, when fame
> Had spread his cursèd deed to the honored name
> Of Pericles, to rage the city turn,
> That him and his they in his palace burn.
> The gods for murder seemèd so content
> To punish—although not done, but meant.
> So, on your patience evermore attending,
> New joy wait on you. Here our play has ending. (Ep.1–18)

As we would expect, Gower is interested in the moral lessons that the play has to teach about divine justice, with evil punished and good rewarded. We know that romance, while it can present us with terrifying and unaccountable realities, carries the promise of an ending that reassures us that the gods are just and tragic events get resolved. We don't mind hearing a quick catalogue of retrospection, though we may be slightly amused when Gower gets to Cleon and stumbles a bit. Cleon was not complicit in Marina's murder; he was appalled by it. And it wasn't really a murder, as things turned out ("not done, but meant"). So the moral lesson blurs a bit and Gower winds up quickly. His last five words could not be more succinct.

There is a widespread assumption, as mentioned earlier, that parts of the play are by George Wilkins, who was collaborating with Shakespeare. That may be true for some of the scenes in the first two acts, though I don't find it especially persuasive. The problem is that commentators, once they have dismissed the first two acts as a collaborator's work, feel free to ignore Gower and his tremendous significance, both for this story and for the rest of the romances. It is the old issue of not seeing the forest for the trees. The play gets devalued and its significant theatrical choices get ignored.

For me, the combination of Shakespeare and Gower can pretty much account for this play, problems of textual transmission aside. But for the purposes of this discussion I need only assert that Gower and his choruses are so central to the conception of the play and to the project of staging narrative romances that would continue to occupy Shakespeare for the next few years that there can be no dismissing the choruses and their effect as somebody else's idea. Gower is quaint, Gower is clumsy. Gower represents the past both in its virtues and its limitations. He carries an old story that he cherishes and manages to share it with us, with results that are deeply moving. Like the chorus in *Henry V*, he greatly aids the playwright in staging difficult material and overcoming audience skepticism. And as he himself tells us, he burns like a candle, bringing warmth and illumination to a dark and mysterious world. The result was Shakespeare's most popular play next to *Hamlet*.

8. POWER AND HUMILITY

The Tempest, 1611

If the King in *All's Well* is a figure of power and authority, he has nothing on Prospero, who rules his own island, commands spirits, performs spectacular magic, and controls the plot of the play of which he is also the protagonist. Prospero is an author and he is a showman, and thus he is more like Shakespeare than any of the other characters in the Shakespeare canon. And Prospero really can be said to perform three epilogues. There is of course the epilogue that comes at the end of the play, addressed to its audience; there is the one that he speaks to conclude and then dismiss the betrothal masque he has staged for his daughter Miranda and her fiancé Ferdinand, an epilogue addressed to an audience of two; and there is his farewell to his magicianship, addressed to the spirits he has commanded through his magic. All three of these farewells concentrate, in different ways, on the equivocal power of the magician: in one respect he is more imposing than any monarch; at the same time, he deals in illusion, which undermines the reality of his power and authority.

The masque epilogue is prompted by a small gap in Prospero's almost total control. While the spirits are presenting a dance of nymphs and reapers he suddenly remembers that he must deal with a threat:

I had forgot that foul conspiracy
Of the beast Caliban and his confederates
Against my life. The minute of their plot
Is almost come. [*To the spirits*] Well done. Avoid; no more!
(4.1.139–42)

The abrupt end and Prospero's obvious passion draw the notice of
Miranda and Ferdinand. He needs to do some explaining. What
follows is probably the best known speech in Shakespeare after
Hamlet's "To be or not to be" soliloquy, an impromptu epilogue
produced by unusual circumstances:

You do look, my son, in a movèd sort,
As if you were dismayed. Be cheerful, sir.
Our revels now are ended. These our actors,
As I foretold you, were all spirits and
Are melted into air, into thin air:

He could stop there, of course, but something about the situation
and his own strong emotion prompts him to go further, extending
the "melted into air" toward philosophical generalization:

And like the baseless fabric of this vision,
The cloud-capped towers, the gorgeous palaces,
The solemn temples, the great globe itself,
Yea, all which it inherit, shall dissolve,
And, like this insubstantial pageant faded,
Leave not a rack behind.

Everything that exists is sooner or later going to dissolve, and one
consequence of that is that our own existences are more brief and
illusory than we can easily understand:

We are such stuff
As dreams are made on, and our little life
Is rounded with a sleep.

This insight does not come out of nowhere. It stems from Montaigne and ultimately from Lucretius, and versions of it can be found elsewhere in Shakespeare's plays. It would be hard to find a more direct and eloquent articulation of it anywhere else, though.

Prospero then retreats from the astonishing assertions he has just made. All things shall dissolve? Ferdinand and Miranda, embarking on a life together, are not really ready to entertain such an insight. Nor perhaps is a large part of Shakespeare's audience:

Sir, I am vexed.
Bear with my weakness: my old brain is troubled.
Be not disturbed with my infirmity.
If you be pleased, retire into my cell
And there repose. A turn or two I'll walk
To still my beating mind. (146–63)

Is this a turning point for Prospero? Not exactly. Actors who play Prospero prefer to fix on the moment when Ariel says that if he were human he would take pity on Prospero's enemies in their helplessness. In response Prospero makes a decision not to pursue his revenge any further. That seems to be a turning point for the character and a resolution of his dangerous power and urge to right wrongs, new and old. He will go on to renounce his magic and free his spirits, bringing the story to a peaceable close. The resolution gives the character a complex humanity that makes the part more playable, experiencing internal conflict and recognizing the dangers of too much power.

But this earlier moment of expression of his "beating mind" is the other side of that dilemma and resolution. This is a perspective that sets him off from most other human beings, the product of his studies and his deep understanding of nature. It is the wisdom of the Buddha, of the Taoist masters, of Jesus in some of his teachings, of the Upanishads, and of all the other sages and mystics who have recognized the illusory nature of this world of forms and objects. To have this overarching knowledge and also to be aware of the dangers of his excess of power is what it means to be the fully realized character Prospero.

Commentators have suggested that the insight about how everything shall dissolve may have come through Lucretius, the Roman poet who dismissed religious superstition and argued for a world of constant flux and change. He was expounding the philosophy of Epictetus in a long poem. Such insights can be found elsewhere, but the recovery of Lucretius in the Renaissance had a profound effect on many of its artists and thinkers.

That Shakespeare should have given this insight to this character at this moment is extremely telling. He was in the process of winding up his own career in the theater, and the analogy he proposes between the illusory world of playing and the sleep-rounded dream that is our life feels like an insight arrived at over many years, hard-won and carefully expressed, an analogy that both elevates art and playing to a level where they mirror reality, even as it reduces reality to its true shape and activity, a dreamlike rhythm of creation and destruction that is endless, unstable, and unalterable.

Between the masque epilogue and the final epilogue there is one other great speech, Prospero's farewell to his magic. It is addressed to all the spirits and beings he has had use of and dominion over:

Ye elves of hills, brooks, standing lakes, and groves,
And ye that on the sands with printless foot

Do chase the ebbing Neptune, and do fly him
When he comes back; you demi-puppets that
By moonshine do the green sour ringlets make,
Whereof the ewe not bites; and you, whose pastime
Is to make midnight-mushrooms, that rejoice
To hear the solemn curfew;

and it turns into a catalogue of his accomplishments:

                              by whose aid—
Weak masters though ye be—I have bedimmed
The noontide sun, called forth the mutinous winds,
And twixt the green sea and the azured vault
Set roaring war; to the dread rattling thunder
Have I given fire, and rifted Jove's stout oak
With his own bolt; the strong-based promontory
Have I made shake, and by the spurs plucked up
The pine and cedar. Graves at my command
Have waked their sleepers, oped, and let 'em forth
By my so potent art.

Unlike Doctor Faustus, he has never trafficked with devils and
demons, but resurrecting the dead, the final claim of this list,
takes him beyond what is acceptable for a practitioner of white
magic and may help to provoke his resolve:

                              But this rough magic
I here abjure; and when I have required
Some heavenly music—which even now I do—
To work mine end upon their senses that
This airy charm is for, I'll break my staff,
Bury it certain fathoms in the earth,
And deeper than did ever plummet sound
I'll drown my book. (5.1.33–57)

The decision to forgive his enemies and give up his magic seems to resolve his situation, to dismiss his excessive power, and to bring the play to its happy close. Given that, an epilogue by this character might be deemed unnecessary. And yet he speaks one, in what I take to be a crucial and unusual decision by Shakespeare.

Here's where it will serve me to be anecdotal. I acted in a production of *The Tempest* one summer (1986) in Oberlin; it featured Patrick Stewart, our visiting artist, taking his first crack at the part of Prospero. Because I was part of the assembled crew (I played the tiny part of the ship captain), I was among the cluster of players who stepped back and left him to walk forward to the lip of the stage to speak the epilogue. From my vantage point at the back, I noticed two things. One was that the audience did not know how to take the epilogue, most of them not having expected it. The reaction was never the same on two successive nights.

The other thing was Patrick's struggle with it. He clearly found it harder to know how to deliver the speech than he had any of his other lines. He was in that liminal situation that the actor speaking an epilogue inhabits, and it clearly made him uncomfortable. One night as he passed me after delivering it, he muttered, knowing I was a Shakespeare scholar, "Some day you'll have to explain that speech to me, David." I didn't get around to it at the time. I'll have a try at it now, mainly for my own enlightenment, as I think Sir Patrick has long since worked it out successfully, in subsequent productions.

When Prospero steps forward to speak directly to the audience, partly in his own person as a retiring magician, partly in the person of the actor who has played him, he adds a new dimension to the performance, one which is familiar to those who know Shakespeare's choruses and epilogues. He enlists the imaginative collaboration of the audience, insisting that their help is necessary to the work of art's true completion, even to absolution or something very like it:

Now my charms are all o'erthrown,
And what strength I have's mine own,
Which is most faint. Now, 'tis true,
I must be here confined by you,
Or sent to Naples. Let me not,
Since I have my dukedom got
And pardoned the deceiver, dwell
In this bare island by your spell,
But release me from my bands
With the help of your good hands.
Gentle breath of yours my sails
Must fill or else my project fails,
Which was to please.

The tetrameter verse couplets are like those of Puck at the end of
A Midsummer Night's Dream, and they prepare us for an apology
that is also an affirmation of the imagination and of playing and
theater.

First there is the reversal of power that is familiar from *All's
Well*. As Prospero becomes helpless, the audience is endowed
with some of his power. They need to return him to his dukedom
by their imaginative completion of his tale. Their applause will
release him, as he released Ariel from imprisonment in a cloven
pine, and will create a breath, a wind, that will enable the ship on
its voyage. His project was modest—not to instruct or moralize,
but simply to please, as good theater can be gratifying and plea-
surable despite, or perhaps even because of, its ephemeral nature.

Now Prospero ups the ante, and this may have been what
puzzled Patrick Stewart most, as it is an unexpected move:

Now I want
Spirits to enforce, art to enchant;
And my ending is despair,

Unless I be relieved by prayer,
Which pierces so that it assaults
Mercy itself and frees all faults.
As you from crimes would pardoned be,
Let your indulgence set me free. (Ep.1–20)

Instead of saying that the players aim to please and will continue to do so, he suggests that he is in danger of despair, a condition that requires the help of prayer and the employment of mercy. Some members of the audience might nod knowingly, having heard that magicians and necromancers, on their deathbeds, would beg for the prayers of others to help save them from damnation. In theatrical terms, *Doctor Faustus* might come to mind.

The need for prayer and mercy sounds acute. For a moment it isn't just a matter of player as beggar and audience as king, but something more like the relation of deity to sinner or priest to penitent. The terms "crimes" and "indulgence" compound this swerve into apparently religious terminology. I say "apparently" because while Prospero says he needs prayer and mercy, his mention of crimes and indulgence comes in the form of an analogy. The "As" is crucial: "In the same way that you would hope to have crimes pardoned and receive mercy and indulgence from your Savior, apply that crucial generosity and possibility of salvation to me" is what I take him to say. Not so much that he is a sinner or a criminal, but that the stakes are comparable: life and death, crime and pardon, high matters deserving serious consideration.

Why are the stakes raised in this way over, say, the epilogue of *All's Well*? We can only speculate. If Prospero is more like Shakespeare than any other character, and if this play coincides with his retirement as the resident playwright of his company, we can infer that he is for a moment truly serious. What is at stake is still the entertainment his company offers and the practice of his art over many years and in many genres. Just as Prospero almost inadvertently lets slip his sense of how ephemeral the world of forms truly is, so Shakespeare here, through Prospero, seems to want us to recognize that issues of absolution and salvation are present in theater and playing too. Or at least that the practice of drama may have a comparable gravity and reach. If the audience knows how crucial prayer and sin and forgiveness are to human existence, perhaps they can grasp a comparable meaning in relation to the players and their pastimes.

We do not know Shakespeare's state of mind as he decided to leave London and retire to Stratford. Perhaps his health was failing. Perhaps he felt emptied out after so much writing and so many years. Prospero says every third thought will be his death, i.e. he is hoping to prepare himself for his end, to settle accounts with his creator and face the mystery of what lies beyond death. Retirement is both retrospective and prospective, and while it may include pleasures like gardening and grandchildren, it also means, sooner or later, the end of life. After death are we freed, like Ariel, to suck where the bee sucks, after summer merrily, or do we face something more grim? Neither Prospero nor Shakespeare seems to have a firm or unequivocal answer.

Prospero does not become Shakespeare in this final moment; he is still the character, behind whom the actor and the playwright both stand. But as he also did in his other two farewell speeches, Prospero speaks a truth that can make us catch our breath and nod our heads, even as we burst into applause once more. This is a more emphatic close than in any of the other epilogues. This is the last of them.

And the play itself, in its entirety, is different enough—no known source, opportunities to read it as autobiography, its exploration of the magic/theater connection through the arts of illusion—that we may be permitted to think of it as an epilogue in and of itself, an epilogue (figurative rather than literal) to Shakespeare's career in the theater, liminal in the sense that he turns back, on the threshold of his retirement, to utter (again, avoiding anything too direct and obvious) his moving and memorable farewell, to his audience, his fellow players, and the world of salvation and forgiveness.

9. Behind the Mask

Will Shakespeare?

Some writers' lives are intimately bound up with their output, quite often in a way that we find enhancing (e.g. Keats, Yeats), or at least satisfying. We are naturally curious about people who create extraordinary poems, plays, or novels. Some, like Homer, are too distant in time, and we must accept that distance as a corollary to their greatness. It's evident too that dramatists may be more elusive than, say, lyric poets. Sophocles is harder to discern in his plays than Sappho in her lyric poems. Like novelists, dramatists tend to disperse their attitudes and emotions among their characters and thus come to life for us, like Jane Austen, in part through their choice of plots and the interactions of their characters.

Shakespeare's elusiveness is legendary. In one sense, we know a lot about him because we have his thirty-seven or so plays, which are widely available for study, performance, and general admiration. But we are nagged by a feeling that we cannot easily grasp the individual who was their creator. It is difficult to separate him from his work, to gain a sense of his existence as a private individual. It is never easy to say what he believed, felt, experienced, as a husband, father, citizen, worshipper, or player. If we compare him with his contemporary rival, Ben Jonson, about whom we also know a great deal, the discrepancy is more obvious. Both were vigorous and productive authors in their time, well known and admired. No one, as far as I know, has ever doubted Ben Jonson's authorship of his own plays and poems. That Shakespeare has been subjected to just such doubt is, I think, further evidence of how he tantalizes us. Frustrated by his mystery, conspiracy theorists try to prove that he was really the Earl of Oxford, or Francis Bacon, or Christopher Marlowe.

Conspiracy theory does not solve the problem. It merely compounds it and shades it over into absurdity by the idea that our greatest author was really somebody else, successfully concealing his identity over an entire career and far into the centuries that followed.

But that the conspiracy fringe exists as a response to the man's peculiar invisibility is also, perhaps, enlightening. Even in the sonnets, which probably contain significant autobiographical elements, we find it hard to capture and describe the person who authored them, wondering how much of what they express is rhetoric, invention, and playfulness, rather than personal experience and emotion. The argument about that continues and will almost certainly remain unresolved.

The situation I am describing has inevitably produced its own robust industry. Biographies of Shakespeare abound, despite and perhaps even because of the frustrations of limitation. We have the plays and poems, and we have the few known facts about the life of this man, who grew up in Stratford, moved to London to become an actor, playwright, and part owner of a theater and theater company, prospered substantially and then retired back to his hometown, where he died and was buried. Biographers must speculate on the meaning of these sketchy details while also exploring the plays and poems for further understanding of the man and his life.

For my part, the biography I admire most is the one by Jorge Luis Borges, the great Argentine fabulist. It is called "Everything and Nothing," and over its short course, two pages, it suggests that Shakespeare felt an inner emptiness, an existential absence of self that he filled by becoming, as a writer and actor, all the characters of his invention. He fought "the hated flavor of unreality" throughout his career:

> *History adds that before or after dying he found himself in the presence of God and told Him: "I who have been so many men in vain want to be one and myself." The voice of the Lord answered from a whirlwind: "Neither am I anyone; I have dreamt the world as you dreamt your work, my Shakespeare, and among the forms in my dream are you, who like myself are many and no one."*

"History adds," claims Borges dryly, when of course it adds no such thing. Borges is winding up a parable, based on the fact that an author who is somehow everywhere and nowhere, everyone and no one, does indeed begin to seem godlike. Hence, he implies, Shakespeare's special standing as an icon, a culture hero like none other, who gets to converse with God, a fellow maker. His summary, brief as it is, accounts both for the greatness and for the elusiveness. It also teases the phenomenon called Bardolatry, and that feature of our response is what drives some people crazy and leads to the conspiracy theories.

Perhaps it takes a great writer to know another great writer. Borges' own fascination with the infinite and his almost godlike perspectives on human life may be viewed in a mirror here. Another mirror, as I've suggested, and as W.H. Auden confirmed, is *The Tempest*.

*

These observations about the problem of the relation between the author and his work are by way of exploring a summary and conclusion for this study. Because the epilogues are a relatively rare practice for this playwright, their small number can attract us and intrigue us. I believe they offer us valuable glimpses of Shakespeare, at work in his craft and among his company of actors. As we have seen, they may be celebratory (always slyly so, though); they may challenge the audience to a less predictable or perfunctory response; and they may reflect the playwright's thinking about the meaning of playing, acting, and pretending. What we can learn about Shakespeare from his epilogues does not revolutionize our picture of him. But it does bring us useful insights into his development and clarification of his thoughts about his art, including his thoughts as he moved into retirement.

Most notable, perhaps, is the fact that the epilogues are never personal. Ben Jonson might write one in his own identity as an artist, claiming his personal rights in relation to the players and the audience, or reaffirming his pride of authorship. Shakespeare, on the other hand, speaks through his characters, and not for himself but for the company and, more generally, for the value of art. In one way that confirms Borges' portrait of him, but in another sense it exposes the romanticizing that Borges and others have indulged in. Emphasizing the man's sense of solitude ignores his daily and fruitful working relationship with his fellow artists. He may be elusive, but he is never a loner, early to late. He's very much a man of his time and place, aware of fashions and disputes, confident in his artistry without, apparently, being vain. His art, moreover, is continuous with other art: he helps himself liberally from sources like Plutarch or Holinshed, without ever seeming self-conscious about the charge of plagiarism; he rewrites older plays, improving them substantially, as is the case with both *Hamlet* and *Lear*; and he works with other writers and with his fellow actors to find the best choices for his plots and characters. In many respects, he is more like a successful Hollywood screenwriter than a solitary literary genius. He would be astonished, I suspect, at the way we single him out from among his contemporaries.

I took my title, as I've noted, from the first line of the epilogue to *All's Well That Ends Well*. I recently saw a broadcast of a production of that play from the Globe, in London. It was a special pleasure to recall that I once played the King and thus got to speak the lines of that epilogue. I remember well that saying them connected me with the audience in a new way, and that they allowed me to speak for the company of actors in a gratifying fashion: we had, after all, worked hard together to bring this off. What else those words suggested, and anticipated, I have explored in the previous chapters. They lead, I think, to Prospero and his three great farewells. The epilogues may confirm Shakespeare's relative reticence, but they also reveal him at work, enjoying the company of his fellow actors and his complicated relations with his audiences.

In the Globe production, for reasons I could not fathom, the epilogue was given to another actor than the King. Then the actor who had played the King led the company in a vigorous and spirited bout of dancing, not specified in Shakespeare's text, but a conclusion we know was a common practice by his company. In this case the dance reminded us of the way the king has been cured of his wasting disease, as well as all the skill we had witnessed among the actors. The dance helped clear the air, as did the epilogue, after an equivocal dramatic resolution.

As I have argued, when an actor speaks an epilogue he/she is in a liminal space, poised on a threshold: no longer exactly the character in the play and not quite yet the actor who takes off the costume and makeup and goes home. In this space and moment, identity is at risk, as is judgment on the performance just concluded. The audience shares that liminality and risk with the actor, the company, and the playwright. All are involved for a moment in a glance back, a special perspective on art, performance, and meaning. I think Shakespeare, as playwright and actor, and as master of indirection, understood and valued that liminal moment. I believe that this examination of his epilogues has helped to demonstrate how his sense of the transition functioned in relation to the choices he made as he pursued his career, and in the distinctive development of his art.

APPENDIX I: FLETCHER'S EPILOGUES

1. *Henry VIII*, or *All Is True* (1613)

Shakespeare had probably retired back to Stratford and was certainly far less active with his company when this last of his history plays was written and performed in 1613. It is famous for causing, at one performance in June of that year, a fire that burned the Globe to the ground. I take it to be one of a group of three, the others being *The Two Noble Kinsmen* and the lost *Cardenio*, that Shakespeare produced for the company in collaboration with John Fletcher, who was in the process of replacing him as the resident playwright. Shakespeare's withdrawal from the busy life of writing and performing was marked, we might surmise, by his supervising Fletcher's apprenticeship. He was naturally less involved, both literally and figuratively, and readers can sense the difference. While some have tried to make the case that this play, along with *The Two Noble Kinsmen*, represents a culminating vision from the playwright, allying it with the late romances, most commentators find it uneven and, next to the earlier histories, unimpressive. There's some superb writing, but at the play's center is a cipher, King Henry, whom Shakespeare and Fletcher are either unwilling or unable (fearing censorship) to characterize effectively. That absence at the center affects other characterizations and tends to turn the play into a processional or pageant. It is not as negligible as one critic's dismissal of it as "patriotic piffle," perhaps, but well below the high standard we have for Shakespeare, early to late.

For my purposes here, however, questions of authorship and commitment to the project need only be focused on the epilogue. I have two observations: 1. It matches the prologue in trying to tease the audience into a compliant response. 2. It is probably not the work of Shakespeare, although it has a very Shakespearean element.

Doctor Johnson thought both the prologue and epilogue to be the work of Ben Jonson, and while that is plausible on the grounds of style and tone, it is unlikely in other ways. Much more likely is that the author is Fletcher, co-author of the play, and that he is imitating Jonson's manner. But let's keep our possibilities open for now.

Here are the opening lines of the prologue:

> I come no more to make you laugh. Things now
> That bear a weighty and a serious brow,
> Sad, high and working, full of state and woe,
> Such noble scenes as draw the eye to flow,
> We now present. Those that can pity here
> May—if they think it well—let fall a tear:
> The subject will deserve it. Such as give
> Their money out of hope they may believe
> May here find truth too.

"Truth" is an issue in this play, which purports to be faithful to historical events, a fidelity to history that comes out, as I've suggested, feeling fairly superficial. But the message to the audience is clear: these are important and grave moments in the history of the nation, and they are being carefully represented. Those who pay more, for better seating, are thought to be judicious, and it is suggested that they will be well disposed:

> Those that come to see
> Only a show or two and so agree
> The play may pass, if they be still and willing
> I'll undertake may see away their shilling
> Richly in two short hours.

Next, because there was a farce about Henry VIII's reign, *When You See Me, You Know Me*, featuring the King's jester, Will Sommers, the prologue, following up on its opening sentence, finds it necessary to forestall expectations of similar treatment:

> Only they
> That come to hear a merry, bawdy play,
> A noise of targets, or to see a fellow
> In a long motley coat guarded with yellow,
> Will be deceived.

It's a matter of good taste, discrimination, and also of accuracy, of "chosen truth":

> For, gentle hearers, know
> To rank our chosen truth with such a show
> As fool and fight is, beside forfeiting
> Our own brains and the opinion that we bring
> To make that only true we now intend,
> Will leave us never an understanding friend.

The syntax leaves a good deal to be desired, but the message is consistent.

> Therefore, for goodness' sake, and as you are known
> The first and happiest hearers of the town,
> Be sad as we would make ye.

Some flattery does no harm. If this audience thinks well of themselves, they will think well of the play:

> Think ye see
> The very persons of our noble story
> As they were living; think you see them great
> And followed with the general throng and sweat
> Of thousand friends; then, in a moment, see
> How soon this mightiness meets misery;
> And if you can be merry then, I'll say
> A man may weep upon his wedding day. (Pro.1–32)

Authentic history, true re-creation, is the claim. It will be sad,
moving, and memorable. Greatness will be shown to be ephemeral. The stage is set.

Could this lengthy prologue be the work of Shakespeare? It is
certainly possible, but it seems quite uncharacteristic, even when
set next to the choruses of *Henry V*. Shakespeare's prologues are a
good deal more succinct, even laconic, compared to this one. And
late choral appearances, varying from Gower in *Pericles* through
Time in *The Winter's Tale* and on to Prospero's own utterances
as a kind of chorus to *The Tempest*, are more carefully integrated
with the action, characters, and story. If Shakespeare did write
this, he did something out of character. That's always possible,
but the flourishes and tone of this piece, which Doctor Johnson
rightly characterized as Jonsonian, are more likely the work of
his younger collaborator, under the influence of the Jonsonian
aesthetic.

Now for the epilogue, which seems to come from the same
hand:

> 'Tis ten to one this play can never please
> All that are here. Some come to take their ease

And sleep an act or two—but those, we fear,
We've frighted with our trumpets, so 'tis clear
They'll say 'tis naught. Others to hear the city
Abused extremely and to cry, "That's witty!"—
Which we have not done neither—that I fear
All the expected good we're like to hear
For this play at this time is only in
The merciful construction of good women,
For such a one we showed 'em. If they smile
And say 'twill do, I know within a while
All the best men are ours—for 'tis ill hap
If they hold when their ladies bid 'em clap. (Ep.1–14)

The tone of teasing, picking out segments of the audience that are less astute or attentive, would seem to continue the vein of the prologue. Some come to sleep, and are waked by the trumpets (not to mention the cannons that caused the famous fire), while others want satirical treatments of contemporary London life, not this foray into the past.

But the second half of this epilogue swerves in what we might well call a Shakespearean direction: in common with both *2 Henry IV* and *As You Like It*, it makes a special appeal to the women in the audience. Their approval, it suggests, will bring the men along, and everything will be fine. The approval will presumably be largely based on the sympathetic treatment of Queen Katherine, who is given a vision of angels as she dies, sanctifying, in effect, her goodness and personal sacrifice.

Does the swerve mean that Shakespeare wrote the epilogue? Or that he wrote part of it? If two writers collaborate, they can presumably do so even on an epilogue. Or, more likely, we might conjecture Fletcher as the author of it, acting in part on a suggestion by his mentor, about a good note to strike in seeking audience approval. Whatever we decide, there's a momentary flash of connection that ought to intrigue any reader.

My own conclusion is that Fletcher wrote this epilogue, but wrote it under the influence of Mr. Shakespeare, at least in its latter half. "The merciful construction of good women" is, I think, a Shakespearean perception, cherished from a lengthy career in the theater and exemplified by people like the Duchess of Pembroke and the new and old Queens. I can't prove this, but I think it makes a good deal of sense and aligns with perceptions arrived at in earlier parts of this study.

2. *The Two Noble Kinsmen* (1613)

Contiguous in all respects with *Henry VIII* is the romance Shakespeare and Fletcher wrote together, based on Chaucer's Knight's Tale. Some commentators have tried to elevate it to a status comparable with the other late romances, but it does not, in my view, really hold up to such scrutiny. Fletcher is learning his craft, while Shakespeare is detaching himself from his deeper commitments. The result, despite some wonderful moments and stunning poetry, is disappointing. Although it is a romance, Shakespeare would seem to be even less committed here; it's probably significant that while *Henry VIII* made it into the First Folio, this play did not, despite the availability of a reliable text.

Meanwhile, the epilogue, which most commentators assign to Fletcher, certainly doesn't feel Shakespearean. It follows a closing summary speech by Theseus, very much in Shakespeare's late style, so that the effect is jarring:

> I would now ask ye how ye like the play,
> But it is as with schoolboys, cannot say;
> I am cruel fearful. Pray yet stay a while

And let me look upon ye. No man smile?
Then it goes hard, I see. He that has
Loved a young handsome wench then, show his face—
'Tis strange if none be here—and if he will,
Against his conscience let him hiss and kill
Our market. 'Tis in vain, I see, to stay ye;
Have at the worst can come, then! Now, what say ye?
And yet mistake me not. I am not bold;
We have no such cause. If the tale we have told,
For 'tis no other, any way content ye—
For to that honest purpose it was meant ye—
We have our end, and ye shall have ere long,
I dare say, many a better, to prolong
Your old loves to us. We and all our might
Rest at your service. Gentlemen, good night! (Ep.1–18)

The author of this nervous patter is a relative newcomer, anxious
about his relation to his audience and the success of his offering.
Indications are that the play was relatively successful over time;
it appeared in a quarto in 1634 and eventually ended up in the
Beaumont and Fletcher Second Folio (1679). But the audience
sounds fickle, and giving them an old tale feels like a risky enterprise, despite Shakespeare's late successes. We can feel for Fletcher
as he tries his wings and wishes his Stratford collaborator would
help him find the right formula.

He sounds perkier in the prologue, which begins "New plays
and maidenheads are near akin: / Much followed both, for both
much money gi'en." He goes on to brag about adapting an author
as distinguished as Chaucer and to admit to anxiety about living
up to that literary reputation. Again, this does not sound like
Shakespeare ending a career, but like Fletcher, embarking on one.

*

Different though they are from each other, these two epilogues stand apart as uncharacteristic of Shakespeare's practice
and style. They seem unmistakably to have been composed by
his young collaborator. Their contrast with the epilogues treated
in this study helps clarify what is distinctive about our elusive
master. He likes to be indirect, he likes to share his pleasure in
creation with his company and his audience, and he does not
tend to apologize or explain what he has done. He can match an
epilogue to a play, with ease, when he feels one is needed. That
need is rare, but when it happens we can glimpse him at work,
confident and always willing to experiment.

APPENDIX 2: WHO PLAYED WHICH ROLES?

Speculation about casting in Shakespeare's company and its productions properly belongs outside the main frame of my discussion of epilogues, not least because it is extremely conjectural. But considering whether Shakespeare might have cast himself in any of the roles associated with epilogues is an intriguing line of inquiry and I have made some space for it in this second appendix.

We can eliminate several roles right away: Rosalind, Falstaff, Feste, and Puck are not characters we would consider Shakespeare performing, for various reasons. We know that Falstaff was played by Kemp and Feste by Robert Armin. We know that Rosalind would be played by a boy, and that Puck is too youthful and active to be handled by other than a young and quite athletic player.

But what if Shakespeare took the role of the Chorus in *Henry V*? That is a part that we can imagine him playing—until we get to the epilogue. The Chorus's reference to "our bending author" would seem to eliminate him from the role. The elimination is bolstered by the fact that we can dissociate the Chorus's unmitigated admiration for Henry from the author's more mixed and nuanced attitude. Unless the reference to "our bending author" is ironic, we can probably cross the part of the Chorus off the list of possibilities. Or we can say that it's unlikely, but an interesting speculation.

It's more tempting to imagine Shakespeare playing Gower, the author who fronts for the author of *Pericles*. He could also double characters like Cerimon and Antiochus. As Gower he would be participating in a kind of in-joke, adopting the pose of a writer who is both a distinguished historical figure and a rather inept playwright. Unless the role was larger than was Shakespeare's practice by the time he wrote this play—a definite possibility—we can see Shakespeare being Gower and preserving the fiction all the way through the epilogue, which is as Goweresque as anything else in the play.

Now consider Shakespeare as Pandarus. It's a manageable role for him and he could double as Nestor in the Greek scenes. It would make the bitter epilogue just a bit more bitter, casting the playwright as a kind of archetypal pimp, arranging trysts between players and audiences. Some will feel this goes too far, but the speculation helps illuminate the intensity of the play and the impact of the epilogue.

Finally, we have the King of France in *All's Well* and Prospero in *The Tempest*. The first of these roles seems quite plausible for Shakespeare, and while saying Shakespeare may have played the King does not alter the epilogue's force and meaning, where the King speaks for the whole company, there is certainly nothing in the notion to contradict this option.

Prospero is another matter, given the size of the role and its proximity to Shakespeare's retirement. It's a Burbage-sized role, and we are fairly sure that Shakespeare did not undertake such sizable assignments. Tempting as it might be to see the three farewells as spoken by the author of the entire Shakespeare canon, I don't see how we can make a strong case for Shakespeare making an exception to his own practice of playing smaller parts, even in this instance.

The two court epilogues, for *2 Henry IV* and for whichever play was performed at Shrovetide, could well have been delivered by their author. They are a special case, since they are not connected with any character, being occasional and ceremonial. Putting them aside and examining all the other instances, Gower, Pandarus, and the King of France, then, seem to me the most likely possibilities for Shakespeare himself as their original performer, on through the plot and out to the epilogue.

No clear pattern emerges from this trio of possibilities, nor from the elimination of others, so we have to conclude, I think, that the presence of an epilogue is never an indication that Shakespeare wrote it to speak in his own person, himself moving into the liminal space we have said that epilogues create. That conclusion is consistent, I think, with what I have argued for as the typical attitudes that lie behind Shakespeare's use of sources, as well as his development as an artist and member of his theatrical company. He was not interested in airing his own views, independent of his fellow players or promoting his own authorship. That tells us, I think, a great deal about him.

Notes and Further Reading

Any commentator on Shakespeare and his plays not only stands on the shoulders of earlier experts; rather, it is as though he or she swims in a vast sea stretching to the horizon, a sea of analysis, conjecture, performance, and emendation. I cannot document the ways in which so many previous discussions of all the plays treated in this study are a part of my debt. Nor can I detail performances that have shaped my views of the plays and their author. There too, we are speaking of multitudes. There's also the matter of teaching and discussion, and the ways in which they have inflected my understanding of the plays over many years.

What I can do, in this set of notes, is identify some very specific and recent debts while also guiding readers who may wish to delve further into some aspects of my discussion toward books that will carry them there. In doing this, I am being sketchy rather than exhaustive, and I apologize in advance for any omissions that may occur. That sea I swim in is too vast, and I am no marine biologist.

Quotations from the plays, unless otherwise indicated, are from *The Norton Shakespeare*, ed. Stephen Greenblatt et al., 3rd edition (2016).

Introduction

Reuben Brower's study of the tragedies, *Hero and Saint* (1971) is especially useful in considering how and why the tragedies close as they do. Other discussions of the ways that Shakespeare's plays end include David Margolies, *Shakespeare's Irrational Endings* (2012), on the problem plays; Cynthia Marshall, *Last Things and Last Plays: Shakespearean Eschatology* (1991), on the late plays in relation to apocalypticism in Shakespeare's time; and R. S. White, *Let Wonder Seem Familiar: Endings in Shakespeare's Romance Vision* (1985), on the comic versus the romance endings. These studies touch upon the epilogues glancingly, if at all.

Chapter 1

My own book, *Something of Great Constancy: The Art of* A Midsummer Night's Dream (1966), is my main source for the view of this play as a kind of *ars poetica* and forceful testament, playing with oppositions like art and nature, reason and imagination, dreaming and waking, to question them and undermine them. See especially my third chapter, "Bottom's Dream." Also of interest are Elizabeth Sewell's *The Orphic Voice* (1961) and C. L. Barber's *Shakespeare's Festive Comedy* (1959). Subsequent studies include D. A. Rhoads, *Shakespeare's Defense of Poetry* (1985) and Mark Stavig, *The Form of Things Unknown* (1995). Most recently, Bart Van Es, in *Shakespeare in Company* (2013), sees the play as part of a significant step forward for Shakespeare, stemming from his new relationship as principal artist of the Lord Chamberlain's Men, a redefinition of his authorial role that led to new achievement in "relational drama."

Chapter 2

James Shapiro, *A Year in the Life of William Shakespeare, 1599* (2005) gives an excellent account of the Shakespeare–Kemp differences in his chapter, " A Battle of Wills." Giorgio Melchiori, in his edition of *2 Henry IV* for the New Cambridge Shakespeare (1989, 2007) argues that we have three different epilogues, given at three different times (211f.). My own first work on this play was editing and introducing a group of essays on it, *Twentieth Century Interpretations of* Henry the Fourth, Part Two (1968).

Chapter 3

My chapter on *As You Like It* in *The Heart's Forest: A Study of Shakespeare's Pastoral Plays* (1972) explores the play's examination of the pastoral mode and its self-conscious use of "if." Shapiro's chapter in his *1599* book, "Simple Truth Suppressed," is very useful. The best account of the Wilton performance and its likely circumstances and meanings is in Adam Nicolson's book on Wilton House and the Herbert family, *Earls of Paradise* (2008), 139–53.

Chapter 4

Shapiro is also very good on *Henry V* in his chapter "Band of Brothers" (85–103). He notes that the choruses were removed, along with some other material, for the quarto printing of 1600. Because of its relation to the Essex affair, he argues, the play's politics are practically "inscrutable" (90). His suggestion that the play constitutes "the innovative (and for Shakespeare unique) experiment of introducing each act with an extended prologue spoken by the Chorus" overlooks the repetition of the experiment in *Pericles*. He recognizes the value of the choric counterpoint: "what Shakespeare loses in dramatic surprise he makes up for in the tension between what audiences are told and what they see for themselves" (93). Russell Fraser, in *Shakespeare: The Later Years* (1992), is good on the use of multiple perspectives in the history plays, e.g. 49–57.

Chapter 5

The New Cambridge Edition of *Troilus and Cressida,* ed. Anthony Dawson (2003), gives a good summary of the play's issues and the positions of various commentators. One of them, W. R. Elton, connects Pandarus' epilogue to Carnival, its "testament and death" at Candlemas, and to misrule ceremonies and mock-insults (*Shakespeare's* Troilus and Cressida *and the Inns of Court Revels* [2000]). His perspective locates the epilogue as having been specifically composed for the Inns of Court audience, but other commentators recognize its function in the public theater. One of the best comments on the epilogue is by Barbara Bowen, in *Gender in the Theater of War* (1993): "Shakespeare pushes both chivalric heroism and scurrility to an extreme and then insists that they be heard together" (80). Of interest as well are Roger Apfelbaum, *Shakespeare's* Troilus and Cressida: *Textual Problems and Performance Solutions* (2004), and Jane Adamson, *Troilus and Cressida*, in Twayne's New Critical Introductions to Shakespeare series (1987).

Chapter 6

One of the best things on *All's Well That Ends Well* is an article by my friend and colleague Phyllis Gorfain. It's called "Riddles and Reconciliation: Formal Unity in *All's Well That Ends Well*," and it appeared in the *Journal of the Folklore Institute* 13.3 (1976): 263–81. Gorfain uses her knowledge of folklore to connect the riddles that appear throughout the play, especially at the end. And she is one of the few commentators who bothers to examine the epilogue. After quoting it, she remarks:

> The actor introduces himself in his new role, that of beggar, and teaches us our parts. He thus demonstrates the conventions which organize behavior in the theatre and in life. The shifting roles of beggar, king, or actor resemble positions one takes in a game, where one takes turns at playing. Through the reflexivity in dramatic devices like the epilogue and the fool, and in folkloric devices like riddles, we learn the power and restrictions of the parts we act. (277)

She understands the connection between playing in life and playing in the theater, a connection that fascinated Shakespeare increasingly throughout his career. See also David Haley, *Shakespeare's Courtly Mirror: Reflexivity and Prudence in* All's Well That Ends Well (1993): "The King delivers the epilogue in order to reassure us that our common concerns have reached a festive issue … the playwright signals in the most emphatic way possible that the society of the play has been reintegrated" (253). This may ignore the "ifs" in the King's closing speech and epilogue, which make the reintegration more tentative, and perhaps ironic, but it reflects a good understanding of the epilogue's function.

Meredith Skura's *Shakespeare the Actor and the Purposes of Playing* (1993), which I cite in relation to the idea of the players as kings and beggars, is a very useful study that serves to remind us, again and again, that the author of Shakespeare's plays was indeed an actor, acutely conscious of what the profession was like and how the meaning of playing and roles could be used to illuminate the human situation. That Shakespeare had an actor's sensibility and experience is so crucial to a full understanding of his work that it never ceases to amaze me when any actor (e.g.,

Mark Rylance, Derek Jacobi) doubts his authorship. Fortunately that's the exception rather than the rule.

Chapter 7

As for *Pericles* I must mention my own novella, *Imagining Shakespeare's* Pericles: *A Story About the Creative Process* (2011). While most commentators, arguing for dual authorship, ignore the "authorship" of Gower and Shakespeare's choice of him, I'm happy to say that Katherine Duncan-Jones, in her *Ungentle Shakespeare* (2001), picks up on the fact of Gower's tomb in a church Shakespeare frequented and seems to understand the importance of his choice for chorus (202–205). For the case against single authorship in this play, and others discussed in this study, see Brian Vickers, *Shakespeare, Co-Author* (2002).

Chapter 8

My own previous writings on *The Tempest* will be found in the chapter entitled "Rough Magic" in *The Heart's Forest*, and in "Where the Bee Sucks: A Triangular Study of *Doctor Faustus*, *The Alchemist*, and *The Tempest*," in *Shakespeare's Romances Reconsidered*, ed. Jacobs and Kay (1978), 149–66.

Frank Kermode's 1954 Arden Edition of the play continues to be a useful resource. Alvin Kernan's book *The Playwright as Magician* (1979) is quite relevant, as is Jackson Cope's *The Theater and the Dream* (1973). Leslie Fiedler, in his chapter on the play in *The Stranger in Shakespeare* (1973), has a good account of the epilogue on 252–53. The critical literature on this play is touched on in *Bloom's Modern Critical Interpretations: The Tempest* (2011). Bloom collects eight good essays and supplies a fairly useful bibliography. The Stephen Greenblatt study of Lucretius in the

Renaissance that I refer to is *The Swerve: How the World Became Modern* (2012).

As I was finishing this, I found an interview with Patrick Stewart in which he mentions his Oberlin Prospero. He had played Stephano at Stratford and was interested in tackling the role of Prospero: "Then I went to Oberlin College in Ohio and spent two months teaching as an artist-in-residence. One of the things I did was play Prospero in a full-scale production. It was a very, very bad production, with a mixture of some equity actors and a lot of students. But it was there that I really began to form a sense of how I would like to play the role and who I thought this person was." *Shakespeare on Stage: Thirteen Leading Actors on Thirteen Key Roles*, ed. Julian Curry (2010), 215. Later in the interview he stresses the change in Prospero signaled by the epilogue: "No longer a shaman, or a godlike creature, but a frail and vulnerable human being. And to that end—and this really began way back in Oberlin—I tried to acquire a different tone, almost a different voice, during the last speech" (222-23). So he did indeed work it out. And the production, while it had many faults, wasn't quite as bad as he suggests. It had its moments of magic too.

Chapter 9

The Borges biography is from *Labyrinths*, trans. James E. Irby (2000). While Borges' biography of Shakespeare is my favorite, I can recommend several others. Samuel Schoenbaum assembles all the relevant material in *William Shakespeare: A Documentary Life* (1975). Lively recent biographies include Katherine Duncan-Jones, *Ungentle Shakespeare* (2001), Stephen Greenblatt, *Will in the World* (2004), and Russell Fraser's two volumes, *Young Shakespeare* (1988) and *Shakespeare: The Later Years* (1992).

As I suggest in Chapter 10, I would qualify Borges' sense of Shakespeare's isolation with my own sense of his delight in a community of shared creation and his understanding of his art as a partnership. Evidence of this can be found among all of the epilogues, even as we take note of their considerable variety. And we can confirm its historical importance by noting that Elizabethan and Jacobean culture was deeply interested in the question of individuality versus community. Marlowe had celebrated rampant individuality in characters like Tamburlaine, Barabas, and Faustus. But Shakespeare's individualists tend to be sociopaths and worse: Richard III, Iago, Coriolanus, Edmund. An enterprise like the King James Bible, as Adam Nicholson points out in *God's Secretaries: The Making of the King James Bible* (2005), can teach us how attractive the alternative could be:

> Jointness was the acknowledged virtue of the age. Most of the plays performed in Jacobean England were written by more than one writer. A joint translation, by a large number of people, consulting the original manuscripts in both Greek and Hebrew, but relying carefully on much of the work which the sixteenth-century translators had done, was completely concordant with the ideology of the time. Lack of jointness, either through an overweening individuality or through simple dissolution, a falling apart, was considered an overriding error and a sin. (68)

Our own modernist sense of individuality and freedom as leading characteristics of great artists has tended to obscure what should be obvious: that thoughtful men and women sensed great danger in what Nicholson calls "eruptive egotism" and sought thereby to avert it. It is in that spirit, I suggest, that we do best to hear and evaluate Shakespeare's epilogues.

Appendix 1

In my work on *King Henry VIII* I often consulted the Arden Edition of the play (2000) by Gordon McMullan. He notes that both the prologue and epilogue are generally ascribed to Fletcher.

Both *Henry VIII* and *The Two Noble Kinsmen* are treated at length in a chapter of the Brian Vickers book mentioned earlier.

Appendix 2

For questions about Shakespeare's acting, I can refer readers to the Meredith Skura book mentioned in the notes to Chapter Seven. She sees all actors as wounded narcissists, and readers need not follow that thread, but in general her survey of acting in the period, and especially of its various reflections in Shakespeare's plots and characters, is both comprehensive and illuminating.

ACKNOWLEDGMENTS

Many people helped with this book, over several years, providing advice, encouragement, and information. David Walker, David Bevington, William Carroll, Phyllis Gorfain, Ellen Bauerle, Tom Van Nortwick, Newell Young, Margaret Young, Pat Young, Georgia Newman, Nick Jones, and Robert Pierce all helped in quite various ways. So did an anonymous reader for the University of Michigan Press. To all, my deepest thanks.

Oberlin, March 2017